# Contents

| | |
|---|---|
| What you need to know about the National Tests | ii |
| Preparing and practising for the Maths Test | iv |
| Instructions | 1 |
| Test A (Levels 4–6) | 2 |
| Test B (Levels 4–6) | 13 |
| Test C (Levels 5–7) | 23 |
| Test D (Levels 5–7) | 31 |
| Test E (Levels 6–8) | 40 |
| Mental Test 1 Answer Sheet | 49 |
| Mental Test 2 Answer Sheet | 50 |
| Answers | 51 |
| Formulae | 70 |
| Mental Test 1 Questions | 71 |
| Mental Test 2 Questions | 72 |
| Determining your level | 73 |
| Marking grid | 74 |

# What you need to know about the National Tests

### KEY STAGE 3 NATIONAL TESTS: HOW THEY WORK
Students between the ages of 11 and 14 (Years 7–9) cover Key Stage 3 of the National Curriculum. In May of their final year of Key Stage 3 (Year 9), all students take written National Tests (commonly known as SATs) in English, Mathematics and Science. The tests are carried out in school, under the supervision of teachers, but are marked by examiners outside the school.

The tests help to show what you have learned in these key subjects. They also help parents and teachers to know whether students are reaching the standards set out in the National Curriculum. The results may be used by your teacher to help place you in the appropriate teaching group for some of your GCSE courses.

You will probably spend around seven hours in total sitting the tests during one week in May. Most students will do two test papers in each of English, Mathematics and Science.

The school sends the papers away to external examiners for marking. The school will then report the results of the tests to you and your parents by the end of July, along with the results of assessments made by teachers in the classroom, based on your work throughout Key Stage 3. You will also receive a summary of the results for all students at the school, and for students nationally. This will help you to compare your performance with that of other students of the same age. The report from your school will explain to you what the results show about your progress, strengths, particular achievements and targets for development. It may also explain how to follow up the results with your teachers.

### UNDERSTANDING YOUR LEVEL OF ACHIEVEMENT
The National Curriculum divides standards for performance in each subject into a number of levels, from one to eight. On average, students are expected to advance one level for every two years they are at school. By Year 9 (the end of Key Stage 3), you should be at Level 5 or 6. The table on page iii shows how you are expected to progress through the levels at ages 7, 11 and 14 (the end of Key Stages 1, 2 and 3).

There are different National Test papers for different ability levels. This is to ensure that you can show positive achievement on the test, and not be discouraged by trying to answer questions which are too easy or too difficult. For Maths, the tests are grouped into four ranges of levels, called 'tiers'. The four tiers cover Levels 3–5, Levels 4–6, Levels 5–7 and Levels 6–8. Your teachers will decide which tier you should be entered for. Each tier has two test papers, one in which you may not use a calculator and one in which you may. Each paper will be one hour long. You will also take a mental arithmetic test. Extension papers with questions above Level 8 are also available for exceptionally able students.

# What you need to know about the National Tests

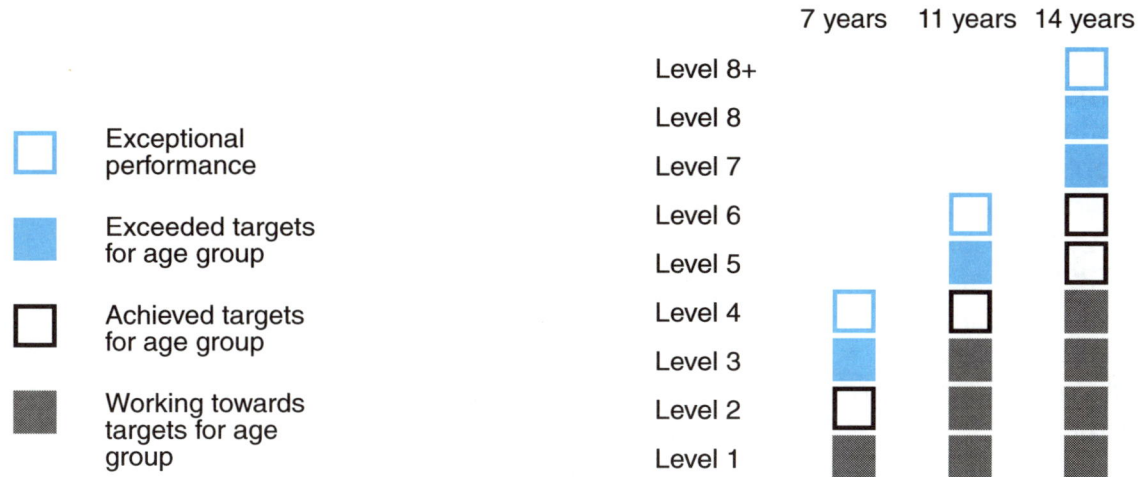

*How you should progress*

This book concentrates on Levels 4–7, providing two test papers for Levels 4–6 and two papers for Levels 5–7. There is also one paper at Level 6–8. This means that you will find plenty of questions to practise, regardless of which tier you are entered for. The bar chart below shows you what percentage of students nationally reached each of the levels in the 1999 tests for Maths.

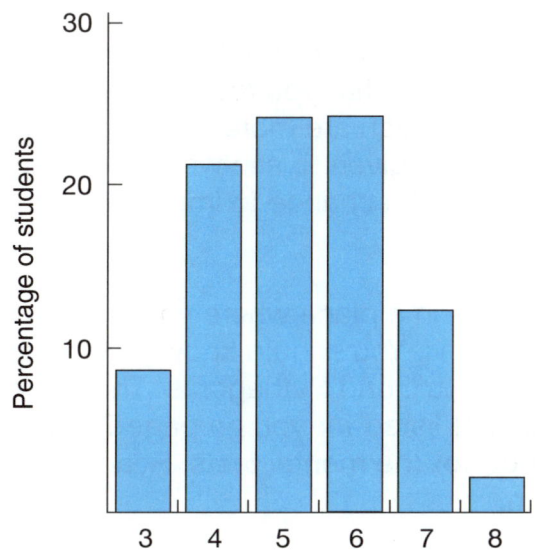

*Levels achieved in Mathematics, 1999*

# Preparing and practising for the Maths Test

### MATHS AT KEY STAGE 3
The questions in this book will test you on the Key Stage 3 curriculum for Mathematics. For assessment purposes, the National Curriculum divides Mathematics into four sections, called Attainment Targets (ATs). The first AT, Using and Applying Mathematics, is assessed only by the teacher in the classroom, not in the written tests. The other three ATs are:
- AT2: Number and Algebra
- AT3: Shape, Space and Measures
- AT4: Handling Data

The National Curriculum describes levels of performance for each of the four Mathematics ATs. These AT levels are taken together to give an overall level for Mathematics. The test papers have questions covering each of ATs 2–4.

### USING THIS BOOK TO HELP YOU PREPARE
This book contains four basic features:

| | |
|---|---|
| Questions: | one non-calculator and one calculator test paper for both Levels 4–6 and Levels 5–7, a non-calculator Level 6–8 paper, and two mental arithmetic tests |
| Answers: | showing acceptable responses and marks |
| Examiner's Tips: | giving advice on how to avoid common mistakes and improve your score |
| Level Charts: | showing you how to interpret your marks to arrive at a level for each test and overall |

### SITTING THE TESTS AT HOME
Try taking Tests A and B (on different days) first. Mark each test to see how you have done. If your results indicate that you are working at Level 5 or higher, then you should try Tests C and D, which are more challenging, sometime later. Work through the answers and advice given to see where you might have done better on Tests A and B. When you've had a chance to improve your understanding, take Tests C and D on different days.

You should carry out the tests in a place where you are comfortable. You will need the equipment listed on page vi. You should know all the commonly used formulae, e.g. for a circle: $C = 2\pi r$, $A = \pi r^2$; and Pythagoras' Theorem: $a^2 + b^2 = c^2$. The only formulae you will be given are listed for you on page 70 and may be referred to during the written tests but **not** the mental tests. Read the instructions on page 1 carefully before you begin.

# Preparing and practising for the Maths Test

Note the starting time in the box at the top of each test. Time yourself during the test, using a clock, a watch, or the help of a parent or friend. During the test, if you do not understand a word, you can ask a parent or other adult to explain what the word means, providing it is not a mathematical word. For example, you could ask someone to explain what is meant by the word 'surrounding', but not 'quadrilateral' or 'decimal'.

After 60 minutes, stop writing. If you have not finished, but wish to continue working on the test, draw a line to show how much has been completed within the test time. Then continue for as long as you wish.

## MARKING THE QUESTIONS
When you have completed a test, turn to the Answers section at the back of the book. Work through the answers, using the advice in the Examiner's Tips to correct mistakes and explain problems. If you required extra time to complete a test, go through all the answers, but do not include the marks for the 'extra' questions in the total scores.

Using the recommended answers, award yourself the appropriate mark or marks for each question. In the margin of each test page, there are small boxes divided in half. The marks available for each question are at the bottom; write your score in the top half of the box.

Enter the total number of marks for each question on the Marking Grid on page 74. Then add them up to find the total for the test. Look at the Level Charts on page 73 to determine your level for each test, as well as an overall level.

If you have achieved at least Level 6 in Tests A–D, try Test E which is intended for assessing Levels 6 to 8. This test should also should take 60 minutes. Again total your marks on the grid on page 74 and work out your level from the chart on page 73.

## ABOUT THE MENTAL TEST
Working things out in your head is an important part of the National Curriculum. In addition to the two written test papers, there is also a mental test. The test assesses your mental recall and ability to deal with numerical problems, and counts for 20% of the final mark.

Two mental tests are included on pages 71 and 72 of this book. You should get someone to detach these pages and read out each question twice. You then have 10 seconds to complete your answer which should be written on the answer sheets on pages 49 and 50.

# Preparing and practising for the Maths Test

## EQUIPMENT YOU WILL NEED

The following equipment may be needed for answering these questions:

- a pen, pencil and rubber
- a ruler (30 cm plastic ruler is most suitable)
- a calculator, preferably a simple scientific calculator

- angle measurer or protractor
  *The angle measurer is probably easier to use than the protractor, particularly for angles greater than 180°.*

- tracing paper
  *This is useful for rotational symmetry questions.*

- a pair of compasses
  *Use this for drawing circles.*

- a mirror
  *This is useful for symmetry questions.*

## FINALLY, AS THE TESTS DRAW NEAR

In the days before the tests, make sure you are as relaxed and confident as possible. You can help yourself by:

- ensuring you know what test papers you will be doing;
- working through practice questions, and learning which answers are right and why;
- checking that you have all the relevant equipment.

Above all, don't worry too much! Although the National Tests are important, your achievement throughout the school year is equally important. Do your best in these tests; that is all anyone can ask.

# Instructions

Each test should take 60 minutes.

Try to answer all questions.

Read the questions carefully. If you think, after reading a question carefully, that you cannot answer it, leave the question and come back to it later.

The questions for you to answer are in blue boxes. For example,

> **How many 3 litre cans does Asif have to buy to cover an area of 254 square metres?**

Write your answers and working on the test papers in this book.

The ▭▷ shows where you should answer the question. The lines or spaces should give you some indication of what is expected.

Look at the number of marks available for each part of a question. This is shown in the box in the margin, for example,

**1**

In Mathematics, marks are awarded for the method you use as well as the answer. It is important to show your working clearly so you can receive credit.

You must not use a calculator in Tests A, C or E, but a calculator may be used in Tests B and D.

Look carefully at the words you write, particularly mathematical words. Read your answers carefully to yourself and make sure you have clearly expressed what you mean.

GOOD LUCK!

# Test A

**WITHOUT CALCULATOR**

Start ☐    Finish ☐

**1**   cube    factor    integer    multiple    square    square root    sum

**Use suitable words from this list to complete the sentences below**

a   45 is a …………………………… of 5.

b   49 is the …………………………… of 7.

c   3 is a …………………………… of 81.

**2**   Here are some wall tiles.

**Draw in all the lines of symmetry.**

a     b

c 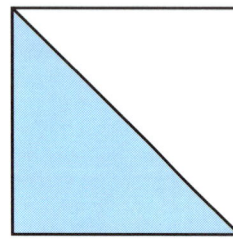    d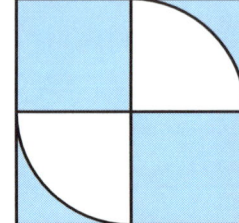

2

# Test A

**3** certain     very likely     likely     evens
unlikely     very unlikely     impossible.

> Use one of these words or phrases to describe the chance of each event.

**a** If I throw an ordinary dice, the number will be odd.

......................................................................................................................

**b** The next vehicle to drive by my house will be a car.

......................................................................................................................

**c** It will snow in London on 1st August next year.

......................................................................................................................

**d** The next king will be a man.

......................................................................................................................

**4**
> Identify the shape which is similar to the shaded shape, and the shape which is congruent to the shaded shape.

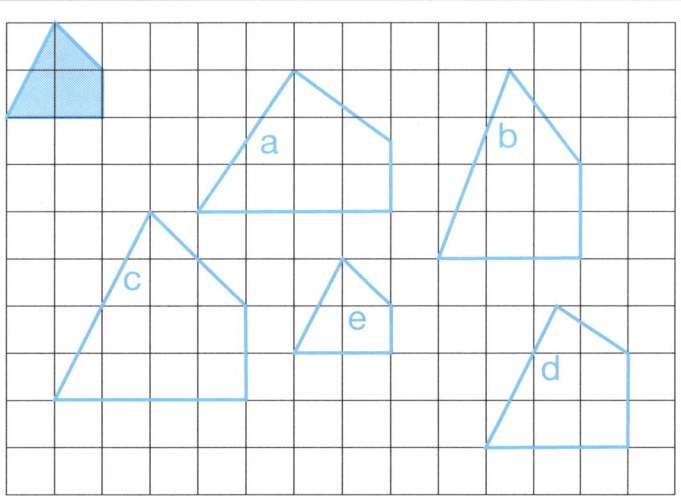

5   Malcolm hired a mixer to make concrete.

This formula shows how much it cost.

> The total cost is
> £9 a day
> plus £15.

a **Work out the cost for 6 days.**

b **Write a formula for the total cost (£C) in terms of the number of days (d).**

c   Malcolm had to pay £96.

**How many days did he have the mixer?**

# Test A

**6** Fill in the missing numbers.

a  486 × 10 = ..................

b  3000 ÷ 100 = ..................

c  217 × .................. = 21 700

d  .................. ÷ 10 = 516

e  .................. × 100 = 40 000

f  32.8 ÷ 10 = ..................

g  0.72 × .................. = 720

h  .................. ÷ 1000 = 0.013

**7a** Jason has a mass of 160 pounds.

How much is that in kilograms?

**b** The picture shows Jason standing by a wall.

Estimate the length of the wall in metres.

**c** How many feet is this?

**d** Jason's milkman delivers 8 pints of milk.

How many litres is this?

8  Here are the results of tests on two brands of torch battery.

|         | Mean     | Range     |
|---------|----------|-----------|
| Brand A | 15 hours | 3.5 hours |
| Brand B | 14 hours | 1.7 hours |

**Which would you buy? Give a reason.**

..................................................................................................................

..................................................................................................................

9  Bob is having a barbecue with his friends.
He wants to buy 45 tins of baked beans at 17p a tin.

a  **How much would this cost?**

..................................................................................................................

The shopkeeper gives him a 20% discount.

b  **How much does he pay?**

..................................................................................................................

**10** Here are 5 number cards

| 5 | 5 | 8 | 4 | 2 |

Use all the cards to make an addition sum that has the answer 600.

6  0  0

**11** Gill has three spinners to use in a game.

**a** Here is the first. It is unbiased.

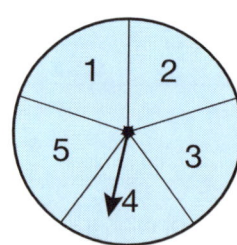

The arrow is spun once.

**(i)** What is the probability that it lands on 4?

.................................................................................

**(ii)** What is the probability that it lands on an odd number?

.................................................................................

8

**b** The second spinner is biased.
Here are the results of 10 spins.

| Result | 1 | 2 | 3 | 4 | 5 |
|---|---|---|---|---|---|
| Number of times | 1 | 2 | 1 | 1 | 5 |

**(i) Explain why the probability of getting a 2 need not be 0.2.**

..................................................................................................

Here are the results of 100 spins.

| Result | 1 | 2 | 3 | 4 | 5 |
|---|---|---|---|---|---|
| Number of times | 10 | 23 | 21 | 16 | 30 |

**(ii) What is the probability that on the next spin the arrow will land on 2?**

..................................................................................................

**c** The third spinner also has five numbers.
Here are some of the probabilities.

| Result | 1 | 2 | 3 | 4 | 5 |
|---|---|---|---|---|---|
| Probability | 0.1 | 0.3 | 0.1 | | 0.25 |

**(i) What is the probability of the arrow landing on 4?**

..................................................................................................

**(ii) What is the probability that it will not land on 5?**

..................................................................................................

9

# Test A

**TEST A** LEVELS 4–6

**MARKS**

**12** Write down (i) the next term, (ii) the $n$th term for each of these sequences.

**a** (i) 2, 4, 6, 8, .................... (ii) ....................  [2] Q12a(i) & (ii)

**b** (i) 1, 3, 5, 7, .................... (ii) ....................  [2] Q12b(i) & (ii)

**c** (i) 3, 7, 11, 15, .................... (ii) ....................  [2] Q12c(i) & (ii)

**d** Use algebra to show the relationship between these sequences.

........................................................................................................  [1] Q12d

**13a** This year, the local football club raised £750 for charity.
It is to be shared between *Age Concern* and *Save the Children* in the ratio 2 : 3.

**How much does each charity get?**

........................................................................................................  [2] Q13a

**b** Last year they only raised £600.

**What was the percentage increase this year?**

........................................................................................................  [2] Q13b

10

**14** Here is the outline of a large house.

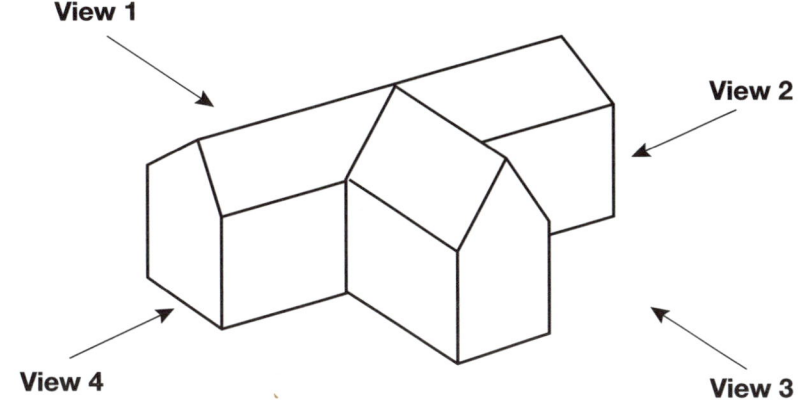

**a** Here is a side view of the house.

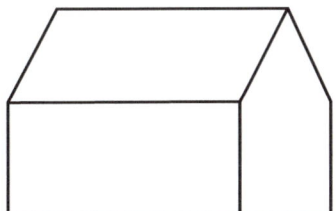

**From which direction is it drawn?**

..................................................................................................

**b** **Sketch the view of the house from above.**

..................................................................................................

**15** These pie charts show information from a survey about computers at home. In the survey 500 people in Brighton and 1000 people in Luton were asked about their use of computers at home.

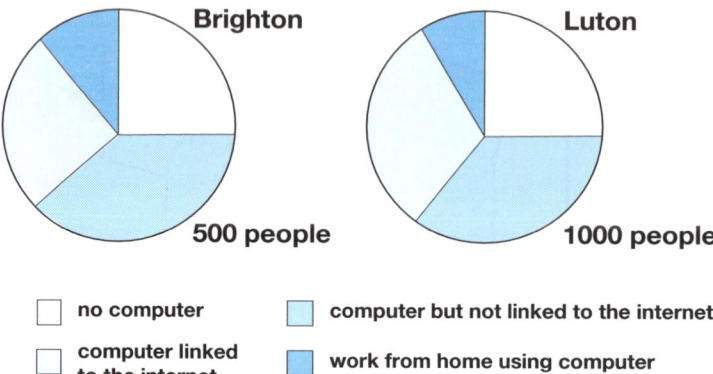

☐ no computer   ☐ computer but not linked to the internet
☐ computer linked to the internet   ☐ work from home using computer

**a** Roughly what percentage of people in Brighton do not have a computer?

..............................................................................................................................

**b** How many people is this?

..............................................................................................................................

Tom said, 'The pie charts show roughly the same number of people in Luton as in Brighton own computers but are not linked to the internet'.

**c** Is this true? Explain your answer.

..............................................................................................................................

**d** What is the same in both charts about the number of people who don't own a computer?

..............................................................................................................................

# Test B

**CALCULATOR CAN BE USED**

**TEST B**
LEVELS 4–6

**MARKS**

Start ☐  Finish ☐

**1** Here are some designs for badges.

Write the order of rotational symmetry under each one.

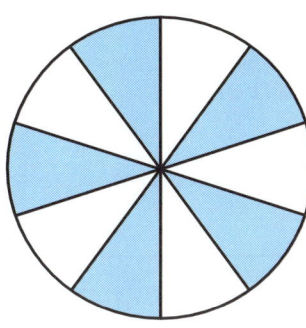

A ....................................

B ....................................

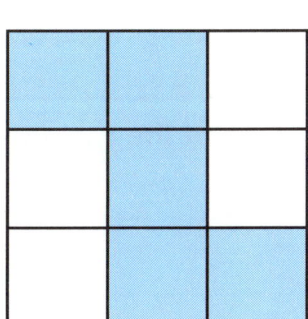

C ....................................

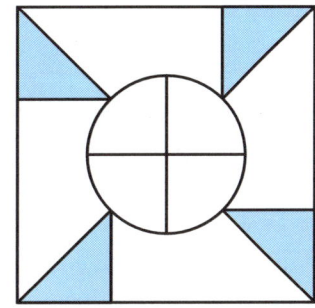

D ....................................

**2** Margaret and Bob went to the farm shop.

**a** They bought 6 kg of apples at 52p a kilogram.

How much did this cost?

£ ...............................................................................................................................

**b** They also bought a 25 kg sack of potatoes for £4.50.

How much did they pay per kilogram?

.................................................................................................................. p

13

# Test B
**LEVELS 4–6**

**c** They paid with a £20 note.

How much change did they receive?

£ ..................................................................................

**d** They checked the prices in the supermarket.

   Apples    78p per kg
   Potatoes  36p per kg

**(i)** What fraction is the farm shop price of the supermarket price for apples?

..................................................................................

**(ii)** What percentage is the farm shop price of the supermarket price for potatoes?

.............................................................................. %

**(iii)** How much more would they have paid if they had bought the apples and potatoes at the supermarket?

..................................................................................

**3** Ranjit has collected data from the pupils in his class.

**Height in centimetres**

| 131 | 133 | 137 | 137 | 138 | 139 | 141 | 142 | 142 | 144 |
| 148 | 149 | 151 | 152 | 152 | 153 | 156 | 156 | 157 | 158 |
| 158 | 159 | 162 | 162 | 164 | 166 | 167 | 170 | 171 | 174 |

**a** What is the median height?

..................................................................................

14

# Test B

**b** Complete the frequency table.

| Height (cm) | Tally | Frequency |
|---|---|---|
| 130 to 139 | | |
| 140 to 149 | | |
| 150 to 159 | | |
| 160 to 169 | | |
| 170 to 179 | | |

**c** Show the information on a frequency diagram.

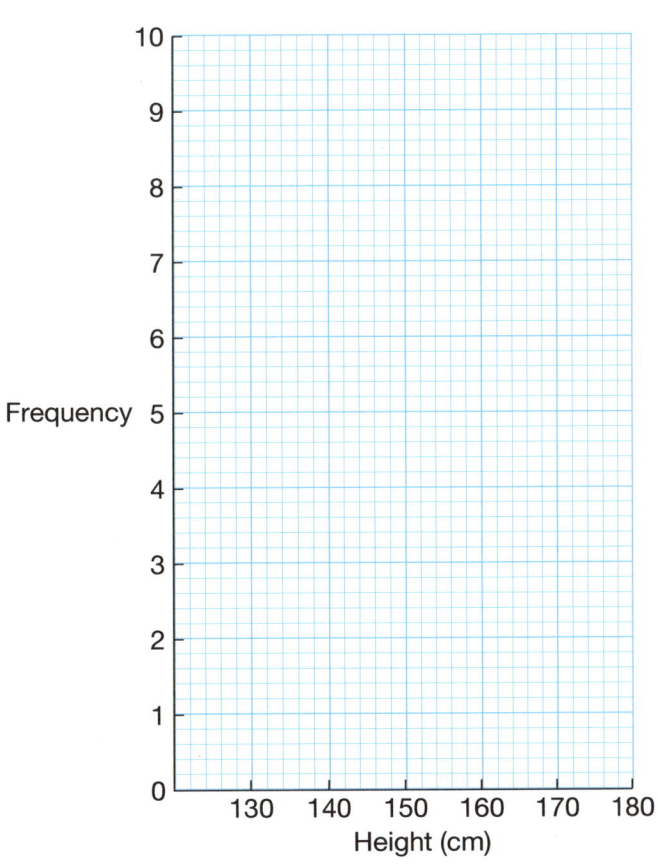

**d** State the modal group.

........................................................................

This diagram shows the heights of the pupils in another class.

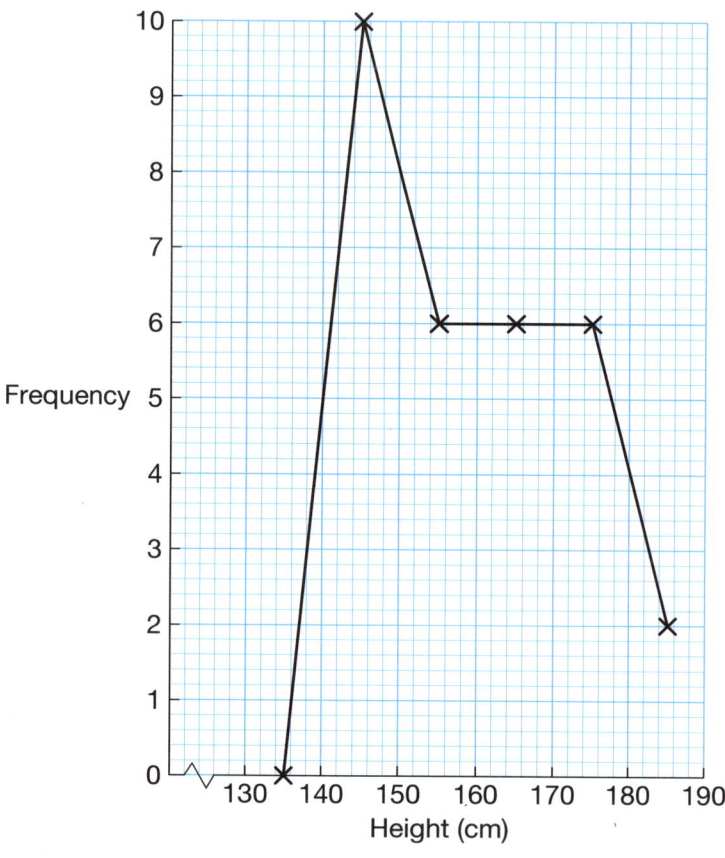

**e** Make two comparisons with Ranjit's class.

........................................................................

........................................................................

# Test B

**4**

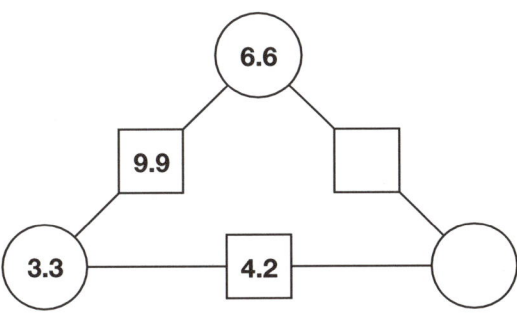

The numbers in the circles along each line add up to the number in the square on that line.

6.6+3.3=9.9

**a** Fill in the missing numbers in the square and the circle in the diagram above.

**b** Fill in the missing numbers in this diagram.

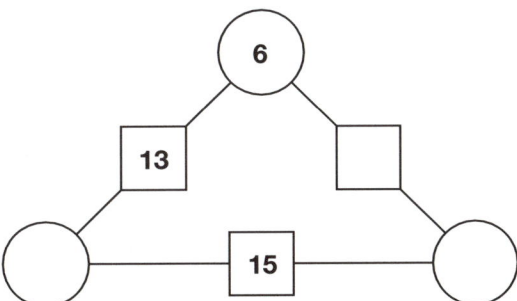

**c** Fill in the missing expressions in this diagram.

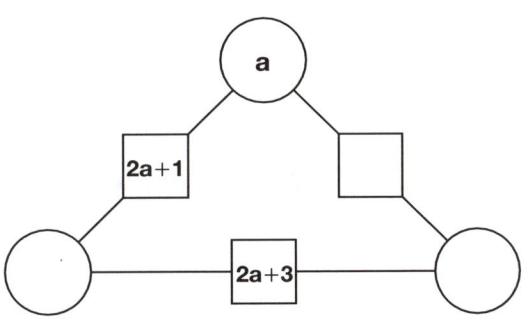

**5** Maureen has measured her garden.
Her measurements are shown on the sketch.

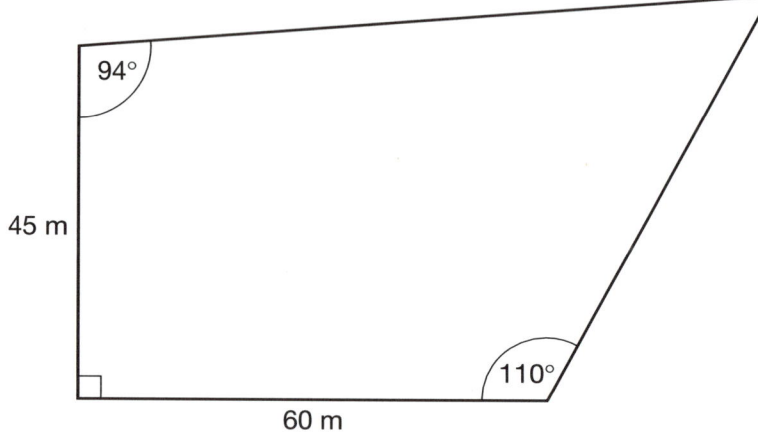

a **Make an accurate scale drawing of the garden.
Use a scale of 1 cm to 10 m.**

b **Measure the remaining angle and sides.**

..................................................................................................................

..................................................................................................................

**6a**

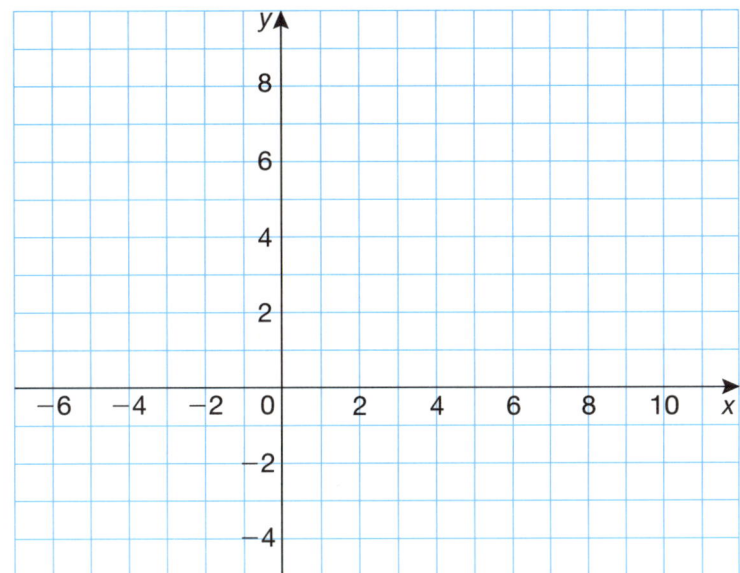

(i) Draw and label the graph of $y = 2x + 1$.

(ii) Draw and label the graph of $y = 3 - x$.

b Write down the co-ordinates of the point where the two graphs meet.

7 Daljit travels 21 000 miles each year on business.
She gets paid 36p per mile travelling expenses.

a How much will she be paid?

b Her car will use 0.14 litres of fuel for each mile she drives.

How many litres of fuel will she need to buy?

MARKS

# Test B

**c** Fuel costs 67.9p per litre.

**What is the cost of the fuel?**

1 Q7c

£ ..........

**d** **Show a rough calculation to check your answer to part c.**

2 Q7d

..........

**8** Electrical fuses are sold in the following ratings:

3 amp    5 amp    13 amp

This formula gives the correct fuse to be fitted to an appliance.

$F = \frac{P}{230}$ where $F$ is the fuse in amps and $P$ is the power rating in watts.

**Which fuse should you fit in a hair dryer with a power rating of 1000 watts?**

2 Q8

..........

**9** **In each part, write the name of the quadrilateral described.**

**a** All sides equal, angles not all the same.

1 Q9a

..........

**b** Opposite sides equal, all angles equal.

1 Q9b

..........

**c** Only one pair of opposite sides parallel.

..................................................................................................................

**d** Only one diagonal is a line of symmetry.

..................................................................................................................

**10** **Solve these equations.**

**a** $3x - 2 = 7$

..................................................................................................................

**b** $4x + 5 = 2x - 7$

..................................................................................................................

**c** $7 - x = 2x + 4$

..................................................................................................................

**11** Tom measures the rainfall each day for 10 days. His results in mm are:
2, 0, 0, 1, 7, 11, 5, 2, 0, 0

**a** **What is the range?**

..................................................................................................................

**b** **What is the mode?**

..................................................................................................................

**TEST B**
LEVELS 4–6

**MARKS**

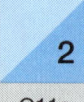
Q11c

Q11d

Q11e

Q12a

Q12b

c **Calculate the median.**

...................................................................................................

d **Calculate the mean.**

...................................................................................................

e **Which average gives the best idea of the rainfall during these 10 days? Give a reason for your answer.**

...................................................................................................
...................................................................................................

**12** Prices in a clothes shop are increased by $\frac{2}{5}$.

a **What is the new price of a jacket which originally cost £50?**

...................................................................................................

In the sale, the prices are reduced to their original level.

b **What percentage reduction is this?**

...................................................................................................

22

# Test C

**WITHOUT CALCULATOR**

**LEVELS 5–7**

**MARKS**

Start ☐    Finish ☐

**1** This rectangle has 2 axes of symmetry and rotational symmetry of order 2.

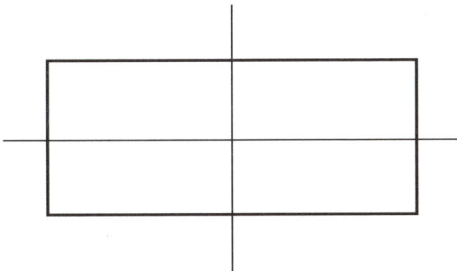

**Describe the symmetry of these shapes.**

**a** A square

..................................................................

..................................................................

**2** Q1a

**b** This hexagon

..................................................................

..................................................................

**2** Q1b

**c** **Sketch a shape that has two axes of symmetry and rotational symmetry of order 2 but is not a rectangle.**

..................................................................

**1** Q1c

23

## Test C

**2** This formula gives the speed of a falling stone.

$$V = 10t - 13$$

**a** Find *v* when *t* = 3.

**b** Find the value of *t* when *v* = 50.

**3** Here are three ways of finding the probability of something happening.

1. Theoretical calculation, e.g., the probability that a coin lands 'heads' is $\frac{1}{2}$.
2. Conduct an experiment.
3. Use data previously collected.

**Which would you use to find these probabilities?**

**a** It is raining while you are on holiday.

**b** Winning the lottery next week.

**c** A drawing pin, when dropped, will land point down.

**d** Your favourite football team will win next Saturday.

24

# Test C

**4** **Solve these equations.**

**a** $2x = 5$

.......................................................................................................................................

**b** $2(x + 3) = 5$

.......................................................................................................................................

**c** $4 - 7x = 3(x - 10)$

.......................................................................................................................................

**d** **Solve this inequality.**

$3x - 2 > 4x - 3$

.......................................................................................................................................

.......................................................................................................................................

**5** Joanna is saving for her holidays.
She saves £15 each week.

**a** **How many weeks will it be before she has more than £250?**

.......................................................................................................................................

Wendy and William are also saving for their holidays.
Their father gives them £20 each.

**b** Wendy saves £4 a week.
After $n$ weeks she has a total of £$P$.

**Write a formula connecting $P$ and $n$.**

.......................................................................................................................................

**c** William's total after *n* weeks is given by the formula

$$T = 20 + \frac{n^2}{10}$$

**After how many weeks will Wendy and William have the same amount?**

**6a** A rectangle is divided into three smaller rectangles and a square. The areas of three of the parts are shown on the diagram.

| 95 cm² | 25 cm² |
| 228 cm² | |

**Find the area of the remaining rectangle.**

**b** Another rectangle has area 1200 cm².
Its width is one third of its length.

**Use algebra to find its dimensions.**

**7**

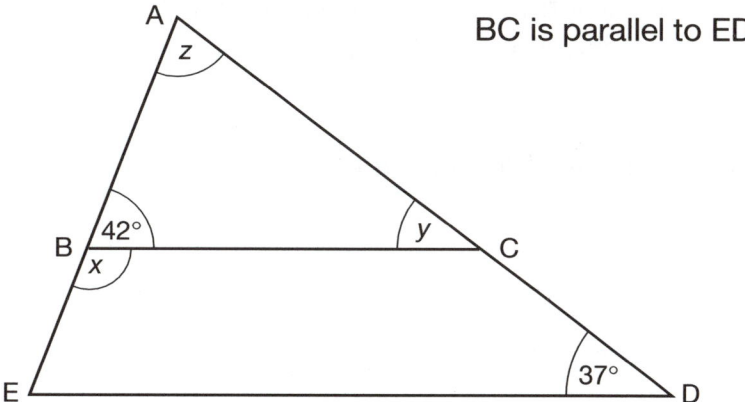

BC is parallel to ED

Find the size of these angles. In each case, give a reason.

a  Angle x = .................... because ..........................................................................

b  Angle y = .................... because ..........................................................................

c  Angle z = .................... because ..........................................................................

**8** Mr Smith has a brief-case with a combination lock.
There are three wheels on the lock.
Each wheel has ten positions, numbered 0 to 9.

a  The numbers to open the lock are 3, 1, 2 but Mr Smith has forgotten the order.

(i)  List all the possible combinations.

..................................................................................................................................

(ii)  What is the probability that he will get it right first time?

..................................................................................................................................

27

## Test C

**b** To help him remember, he changes the numbers.
The first is 1 and the other two add up to 7.

**(i)** List all the possible combinations.

He remembers that no two digits are the same.

**(ii)** What is the probability that he will get it right first time?

**(iii)** What is the probability that he will get it right in three attempts?

**9a** Arrange these fractions in size order, smallest first.

$$\frac{2}{3}, \quad \frac{5}{8}, \quad \frac{5}{6}, \quad \frac{13}{24}$$

**b** Work these out. In each case write your answer as a fraction in its lowest terms.

**(i)** $\frac{2}{3} + \frac{5}{8} = $ ..................

**(ii)** $\frac{2}{3} \times \frac{5}{8} = $ ..................

**10** This trough is a prism with a trapezium as cross section.
The dimensions are in centimetres.

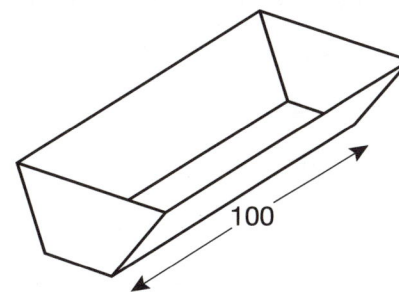
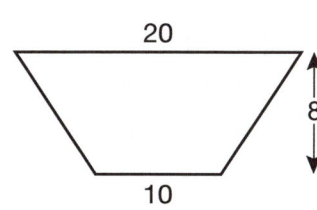

**Calculate the volume.**

**11a** John calculates the value of $\frac{0.137}{0.981}$ to be 0.134.

**Without doing any calculation, explain how you know he is wrong.**

**b** √26 = 5.1    √2.6 = 1.6    to one decimal place.

**Use these to find the following.**

(i)   √260    = ..................

(ii)  √0.26   = ..................

(iii) √26000  = ..................

(iv)  √0.00026 = ..................

**12** Scientists have measured different breeds of penguin in the Antarctic.

| Breed of penguin | Height (cm) | Mass (kg) |
|---|---|---|
| Emperor | 114 | 29.5 |
| King | 94 | 15.9 |
| Yellow-eyed | 65 | 15.4 |
| Fjordland | 56 | 13.2 |
| Southern Blue | 40 | 11.0 |

**a** Draw a scatter graph for these data.

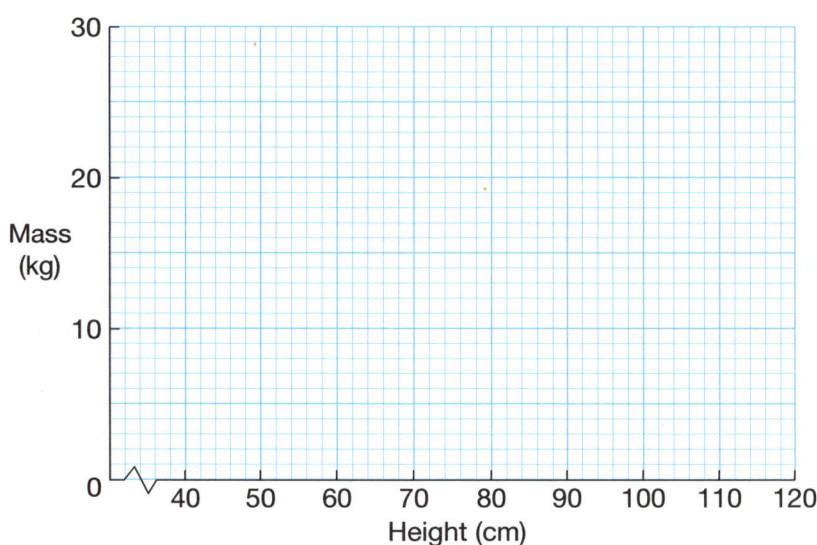

**b** Describe the correlation.

................................................................................

**c** Another breed of penguin has a mass of 19 kg.

Estimate its height. Show how you found it.

................................................................................

................................................................................

# Test D

**CALCULATOR CAN BE USED**

| Start | | Finish | |

**1** Here are some pictures of everyday objects.

**Complete the measurements.**

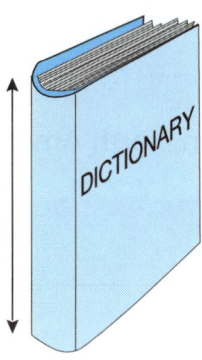

 .................................................. cm          .................................................. m

 .................................................. kg          .................................................. g

**2** These pie charts show how land is used on two continents.

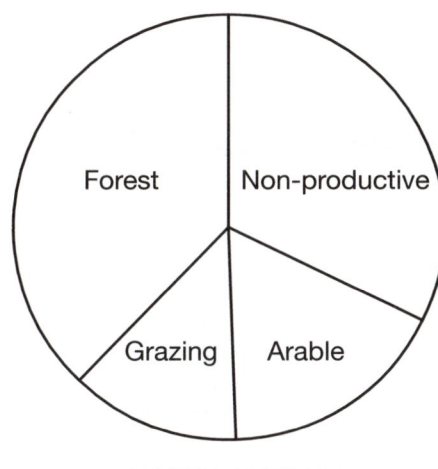

NORTH AMERICA

EUROPE

**TEST D** LEVELS 5–7

**MARKS**

4

Q1

31

a  **Make two comparisons between the land use on these continents.**

..................................................................................................
..................................................................................................

Mark thinks there is more arable land in Europe than in North America.

b  **Explain why this may not be true.**

..................................................................................................
..................................................................................................

3  The diagram shows a rhombus and the lengths of its diagonals.

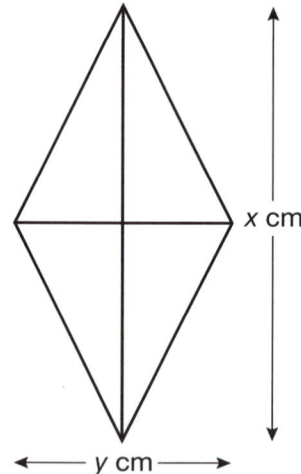

a(i)  **Explain why the area is given by the formula $A = \frac{1}{2}xy$.**

..................................................................................................

(ii)  **Find $A$ when $x = 17$ and $y = 7$.**

..................................................................................................

**(iii)** Find *x* when *A* = 7.56 and *y* = 2.7.

**b(i)** Write down the formula for the perimeter of this rectangle.

*x* cm

*x* + 2 cm

**(ii)** Find *P* when *x* = 24.

**(iii)** Find *x* when *P* = 5.

**4** This window is in the shape of a rectangle and a semicircle.
The dimensions are in metres.

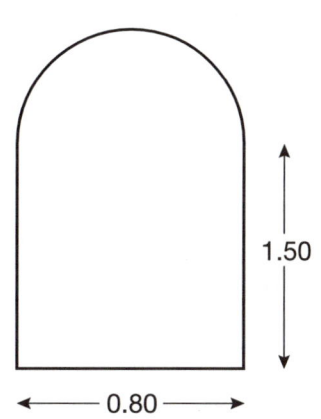

1.50

0.80

# Test D

**a** Change 1.50 m into centimetres.

..........................................................................................................

**b** Change 0.80 into millimetres.

..........................................................................................................

**c** Make an accurate drawing of the window. Use a scale of 1 cm to 20 cm.

**d** Find the perimeter of the window.

..........................................................................................................

**e** Find the area of the window.

✏️ ..................................................................................................

**3** Q4e

**5** A supermarket sells AMAZ washing powder in three sizes.

7.5 kg
£6.59

3 kg
£2.59

690 g
65 p

Which is the best value? Show how you decide.

✏️ ..................................................................................................

..................................................................................................

..................................................................................................

**4** Q5

**6a** A photograph is enlarged to make a poster.
The lengths are shown in centimetres.

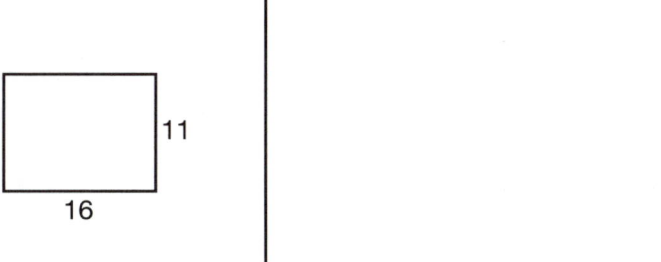

35

**How wide is the poster?**

.....................................................................

b  The photograph was enlarged from a negative. The width of the negative is 24 mm.

**How high is the negative?**

.....................................................................

7  Look at these scatter diagrams.

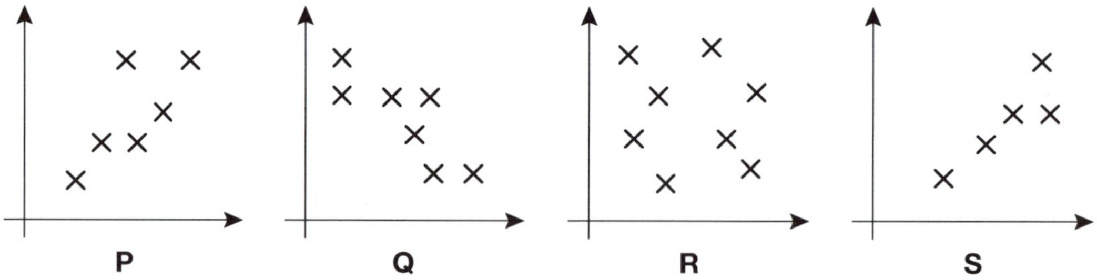

P   Q   R   S

a  **Describe the correlation in diagram S.**

.....................................................................

b  **Describe the correlation in diagram Q.**

.....................................................................

c  Some pupils took both the Mathematics papers in the KS3 Test.

**Which diagram shows their results?**

.....................................................................

**Test D**

**d** Which diagram could show the value of a second-hand car plotted against its age?

..........................................................................................................................

**8** Jo has written down a number sequence. Only the first term can be seen.

2

The term to term rule is +3

**a** What is the 10th term?

..........................................................................................................................

**b** What is the *n*th term?

..........................................................................................................................

**9** The fastest ever drive from the bottom of South America to the top of North America – a distance of 23 720 km – took 24 days.

**a** Calculate the average speed in km/h for this journey.

..........................................................................................................................

..........................................................................................................................

**b** Estimate how long it would take to walk the same distance. Show all your workings and assumptions clearly.

..........................................................................................................................

continue overleaf

**10** The table shows the ages of 120 people living in a block of flats.

| Age | Frequency |
|---|---|
| Up to 10 | 17 |
| 10 and up to 20 | 7 |
| 20 and up to 30 | 37 |
| 30 and up to 40 | 13 |
| 40 and up to 50 | 8 |
| 50 and up to 60 | 12 |
| 60 and up to 70 | 26 |

**a** Calculate an estimate of the mean age.

**b** Estimate the median age. Show how you found it.

**c** The people in another block of flats have a mean age of 35 and a median age of 35.

Compare the two age distributions.

**11** The distances marked on the sides of this triangle are in metres.

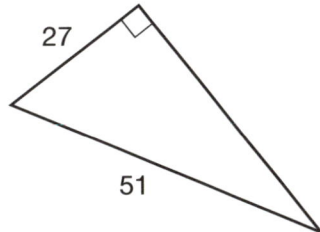

**Find its area.**

**12a** **Solve these simultaneous equations.**

$$2x + 3y = -3 \qquad 6x - y = 11$$

**b(i)** **Find the value of $x^3 - 3x$ when $x = 2$.**

**(ii)** **Use trial and improvement to solve the equation $x^3 - 3x = 5$, correct to 2 decimal places.**

# Test E
**LEVELS 6–8**

**WITHOUT CALCULATOR**

Start ☐  Finish ☐

**1** Pat wants to make a scale model of a tent.
She uses a scale where 8 cm represents 5 feet.

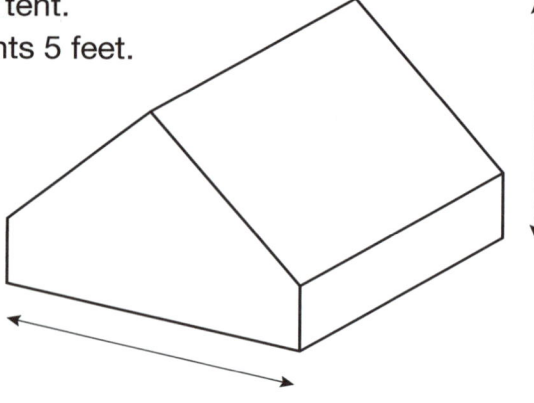

**a** The height of the tent is 8 feet.

**What is the height on the model?**

........................................................................................................

**b** The width on the model is 5 cm.

**What is the width of the real tent?**

........................................................................................................

**2** The mean weight of 10 men is 75 kg.
The mean weight of 15 women is 50 kg.

**What is the mean weight of all 25 people?**

........................................................................................................

**3** Estimate the values of these expressions. Show your working.

**a** $\dfrac{64.7 \times 18.3}{27.4}$

........................................................................................................

**b** $\dfrac{0.73 \times 56.2}{18.7 - 7.9}$

........................................................................................................

MARKS: Q1a 2, Q1b 2, Q2 3, Q3a 1, Q3b 1

## Test E

**4** Jenny has two dogs, Rover and Tiny.
Rover eats $\frac{3}{5}$ of a tin of food each day.

**a** How many tins will be needed for a week?

..........................................................................................................................

The dogs also have some biscuit.
Between them, they eat 600 g a day.
This is divided in the ratio Rover:Tiny = 3:1.

**b** How much biscuit does Rover eat in a day?

..........................................................................................................................

Tiny eats $\frac{1}{4}$ of a tin of food a day.

**c** Work out what fraction of a tin Rover and Tiny eat each day.

..........................................................................................................................

**5** Dillon and Karl are testing six-sided dice.

They decide Dillon's dice is fair.

**a** What is the probability Dillon will throw a 6 next time?

..........................................................................................................................

Karl's dice is biased. He works out these probabilities.

| Number on dice | 1 | 2 | 3 | 4 | 5 | 6 |
|---|---|---|---|---|---|---|
| Probability | 0.2 | 0.1 | 0.1 | | 0.2 | 0.1 |

**b** Work out the probability that Karl throws a 4.

They both throw their dice.

**c(i)** Find the probability that they both throw a 6.

**(ii)** Find the probability that just one of them throws a 6.

**6**

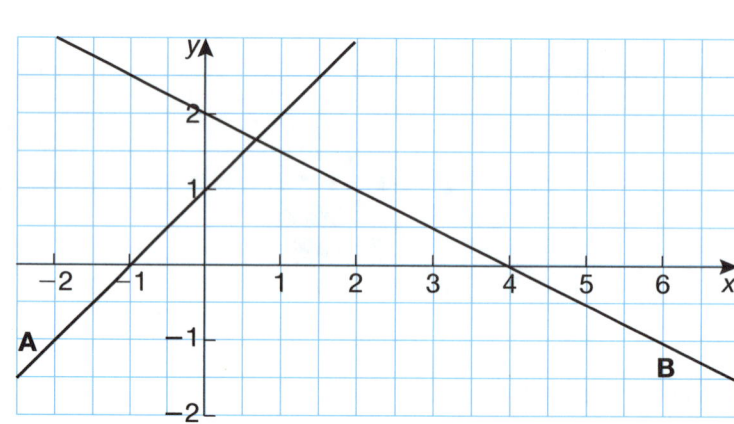

**a** On the grid above, draw the line with equation $y = x - 1$. Label it C.

# Test E

**b** Find the equation of line B.

**c** Use the graphs to solve the simultaneous equations:

$$x - y = -1$$
$$x + 2y = 4.$$

**7** Simplify the following:

**a** $a^3 \times a^2$

**b** $3a^3 \times 4a^6$

**c** $a^2b \times a^3b^2$

**d** $(x^2)^3$

**e** $(a^2bc^3)^2$

**f** $(a^2bc^3)^0$

**8** Two goats live in this small field.

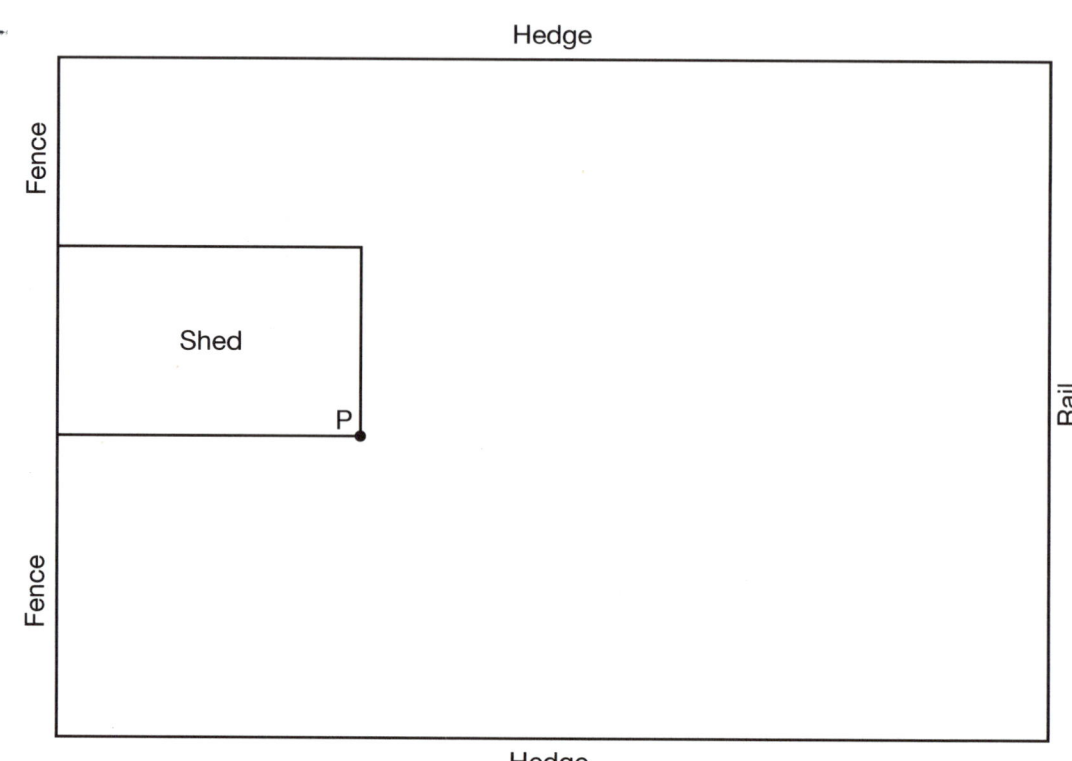

Scale: 1 cm represents 1m

Nanny is fastened to the rail.

Her rope is 5 metres long. The end fastened to the rail can slide along the rail from one side of the field to the other.

**a** Mark accurately on the diagram where she can go.

Billy is also tied to a 5 metre rope.

The other end of his rope is fastened to the corner of the shed at P.

**b** Mark accurately on the diagram where Billy can go.

**c** Show clearly where they both can go.

**9**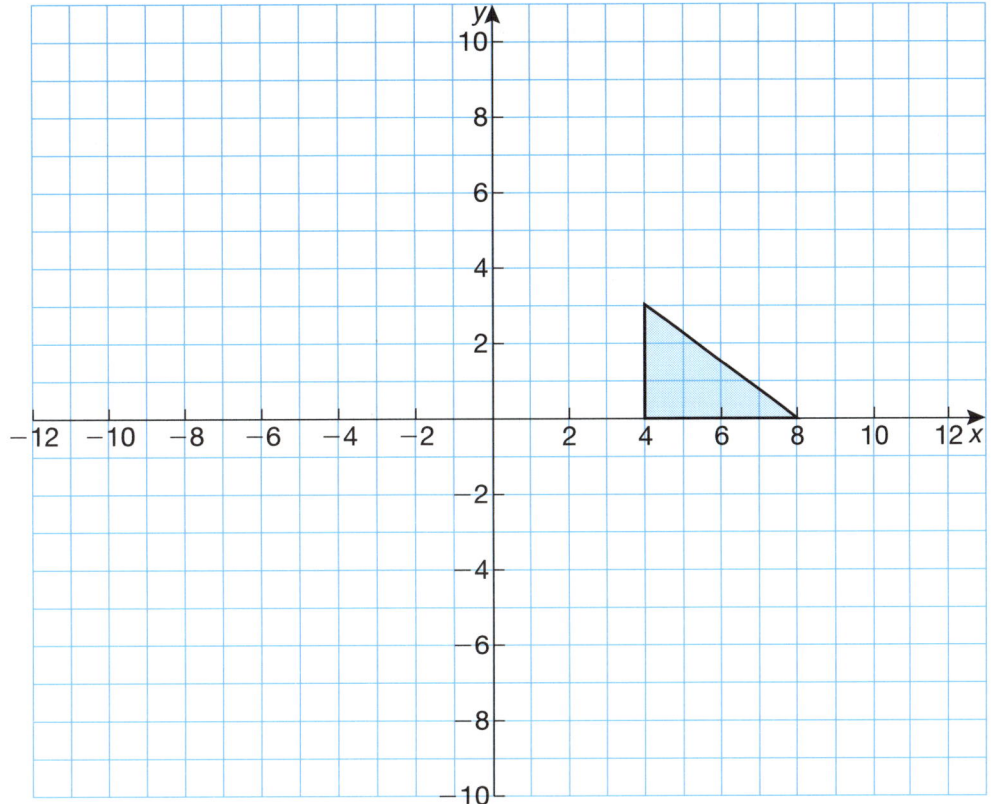

**a** Rotate the shaded triangle about the origin through 90° anticlockwise. Label it A.

**b** Reflect the shaded triangle in $x = -1$. Label it B.

**c** Enlarge the shaded triangle with centre the origin and scale factor $\frac{1}{2}$. Label it C.

**10** Multiply out the brackets and simplify:

a  $3(x - 2) + 4(2x - 3)$

..................................................................................................................

b  $5x(2x - 3)$

..................................................................................................................

c  $x(2x + 5) - 3x(x - 2)$

..................................................................................................................

**11** This cumulative frequency graph (A) shows the numbers of people living in each of 100 houses.

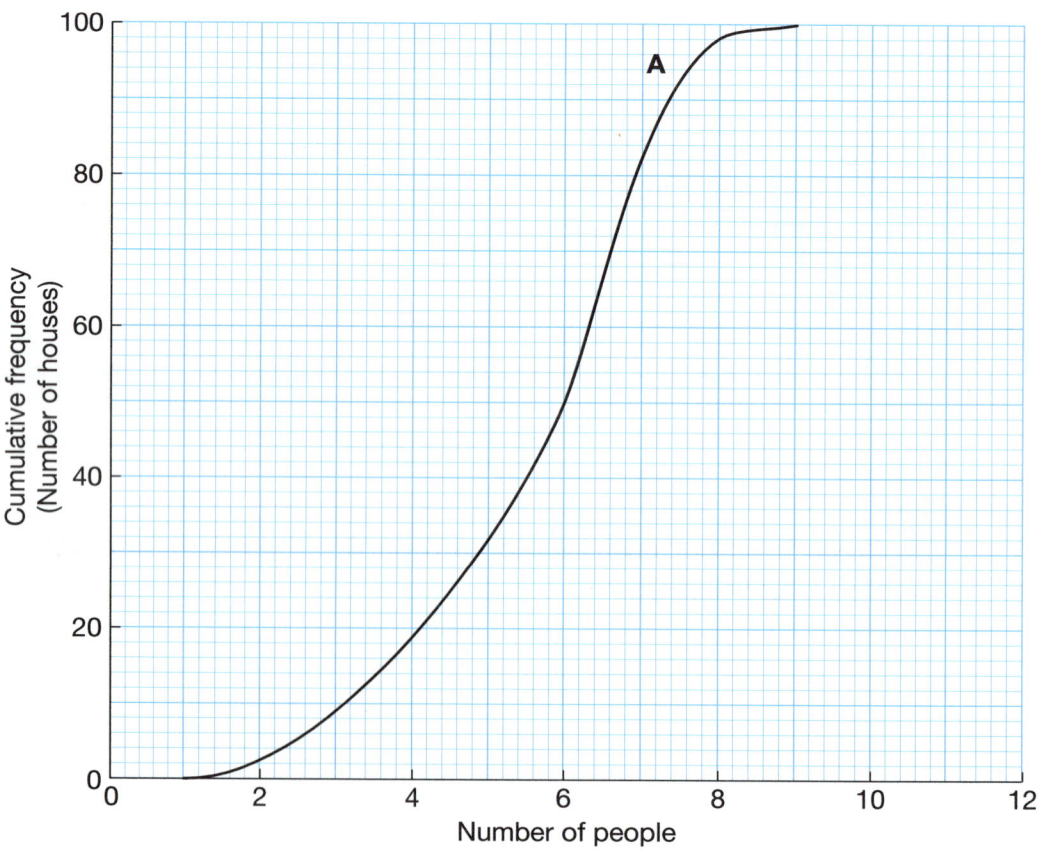

# Test E

**a** Find the median number of people per house.

✏️ ..................................................................................................

**b** Find the interquartile range.

✏️ ..................................................................................................

Here are sketches of six more cumulative frequency graphs.

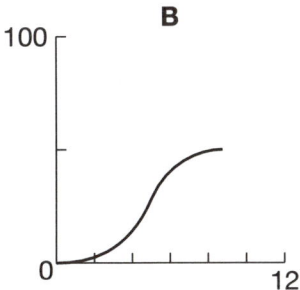
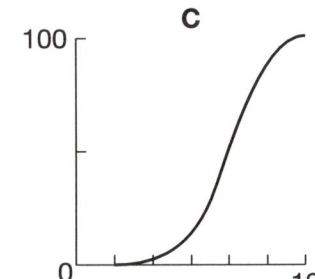
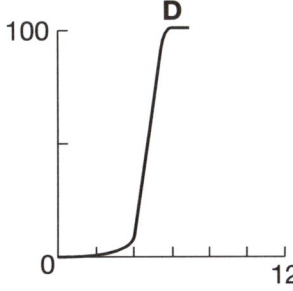
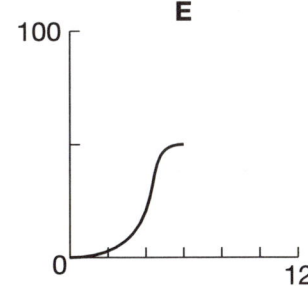
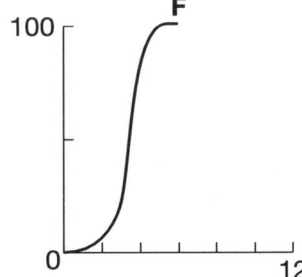
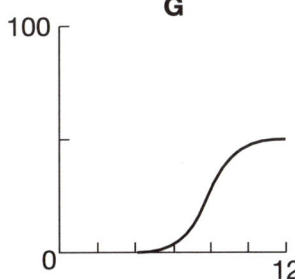

**c** Write the appropriate letter by each of these descriptions.

1 100 houses, lower median than A. ................

2 100 houses, same median but lower interquartile range than A. ................

3 50 houses, same median as A. ................

4 50 houses, higher median than A. ................

**TEST E**
**LEVELS 6–8**

**MARKS**

1 — Q11a

2 — Q11b

3 — Q11c

47

# TEST E
**LEVELS 6–8**

**12** The lengths of the sides of this right angled triangle are $x$, $x + 7$ and $x + 8$.

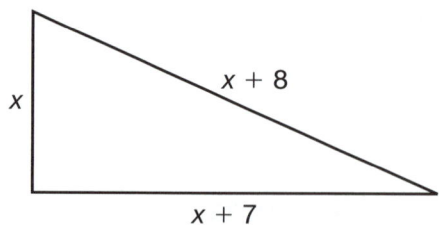

**a** Use Pythagoras' Theorem to form an equation in $x$.

........................................................................................................

**b** Simplify your equation.

........................................................................................................

**c** Solve the equation.

........................................................................................................

**13** In this triangle there is another line drawn parallel to the base.

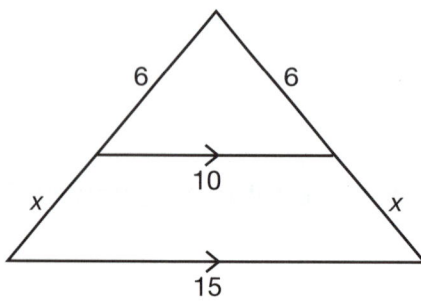

Calculate the value of $x$.

........................................................................................................

48

# Mental Test 1 Answer Sheet

Ask a friend or a parent to detach page 71 and read the questions for Test 1 to you. Each question will be read twice and then you will have a short time to complete your answer. For questions 1 to 6 it will be 5 seconds; for questions 7 to 20, 10 seconds and for questions 21 to 30, 15 seconds. Any data you require is contained in the blue tinted box. **You only need a pen or pencil. You must not use a calculator, ruler or any other geometrical instruments.**

Write your answers on the lines below.

| Q | Answer | Data |
|---|---|---|
| 1 | .................... | 18   37 |
| 2 | .................... | |
| 3 | ....................ml | |
| 4 | .................... | |
| 5 | .................... | 11.15   12.30 |
| 6 | .................... | $2x = 36$ |
| 7 | .................... | $5x - 5y$ |
| 8 | .................... | $247 \div 0.43$ |
| 9 | | 30 mm  30 cm  30 m  30 km  30 g  30 kg |
| 10 | .................... | $\frac{1}{2}x = 4$ |
| 11 | ....................m | 12.5   5 |
| 12 | .................... | 0.2 |
| 13 | .................... | 2%   1000 |
| 14 | .................... | |
| 15 | .................... | 4349 |
| 16 | .................... | $x^2 - x = 0$ |
| 17 | ....................° | 65°   37° |
| 18 | .................... | 5  10  11 |
| 19 | .................... | $2\frac{1}{2}$   80 |
| 20 | | 30 g  300 g  3000 g  30 kg  300 kg  3000 kg |
| 21 | .................... | 25  21  28  17  32 |
| 22 | ....................km/h | 210   $1\frac{3}{4}$ |
| 23 | .................... | $\frac{2}{5} + \frac{1}{3}$ |
| 24 | .................... | (pie chart: Walk, Car, Bus) |
| 25 | £.................... | (cuboid 4 × 5 × 2) |
| 26 | .................... | 0.2  0.1 |
| 27 | .................... | 30  120 |
| 28 | .................... | (right triangle: 5, 13) |
| 29 | .................... | $703 \div 19 = 37$ |
| 30 | .................... | 0.85 |

# Mental Test 2 Answer Sheet

Ask a friend or a parent to detach page 72 and read the questions for Test 2 to you. Each question will be read twice and then you will have a short time to complete your answer. For questions 1 to 6 it will be 5 seconds; for questions 7 to 20, 10 seconds and for questions 21 to 30, 15 seconds. Any data you require is contained in the blue tinted box. **You only need a pen or pencil. You must not use a calculator, ruler or any other geometrical instruments.**

Write your answers on the lines below.

| # | Answer | Data | # | Answer | Data |
|---|---|---|---|---|---|
| 1 | .................... | | 17 | .................... | $\frac{35}{210}$ |
| 2 | .................... | 3.7   1.9 | 18 | .................... | $x < -10$ |
| 3 | ................cm | $7\frac{1}{2}$ | 19 | ................cm | |
| 4 | .................... | | 20 | ................% | £5   £4 |
| 5 | .................... | | 21 | ................cm² | 3 cm, 5 cm, 4 cm triangle |
| 6 | .................... | 0.065 | | | |
| 7 | .................... | 3.017 | 22 | .................... | 7  15  0 / 12  6 |
| 8 | .................... | (cube) | 23 | .................... | 83 × 41 = 3403 / 10 209 |
| 9 | ............hours | 100   50 | 24 | ................m | 75 m² |
| 10 | .................... | 5x − 3 | 25 | ................° | 110°  73°  90° |
| 11 | .................... | 14, 9, 4,... | 26 | .................... | $\frac{3}{10} \times \frac{2}{15}$ |
| 12 | .................... | 10 g  1 kg | 27 | .................... | $3^2$   $2^3$ |
| 13 | .................... | 2:3 | 28 | .................... | $29^3 = 24\,389$ |
| 14 | .................... | 0.05 | 29 | ................s | 3   8 |
| 15 | .................... | 150%   30 | 30 | .................... | |
| 16 | .................... | 1 minute 35 s / 5 minutes 3 s, / 52 s | | | |

# Answers

**HOW TO MARK THE QUESTIONS**

When marking your test remember the answers given are sample answers. You must look at your answers and judge whether they deserve credit. Award the mark if the answer deserves credit. Although you should always try to spell words accurately, do not mark any answer wrong because the words are misspelt.

In the answers below, the calculation is often given as well as the answer. Sometimes the method earns credit (e.g. Question 10b in Test B), but other times only the answer itself earns credit (e.g. Question 5a in Test A). In these cases, the working out has been provided to help you understand how to arrive at the correct answer.

When you go through the answers, try to work out where you have gone wrong. Make a note of the key points, so that you will remember them next time.

Only count the marks you scored in one hour on each test. Enter your marks for each test on the Marking Grid on page 74, and then work out your level of achievement on these tests on page 73.

# Test A Answers

**TEST A** *Pages 2–12*

| | | |
|---|---|---:|
| **1a** | multiple | *1 mark* |
| **b** | square | *1 mark* |
| **c** | factor | *1 mark* |
| | | **Total 3 marks** |

### Examiner's tip
Make sure you do not confuse multiple and factor.

**2a** 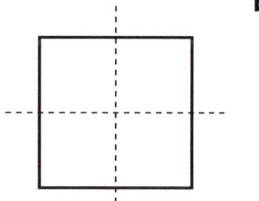  **b** 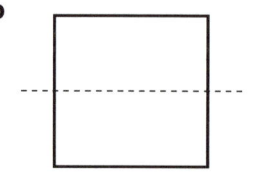  **c** 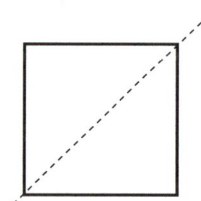  **d**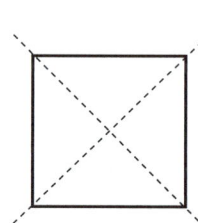

*1 mark each: 4 marks*
**Total 4 marks**

### Examiner's tip
There must be no extra lines drawn!

| | | |
|---|---|---:|
| **3a** | evens | *1 mark* |
| **b** | likely | *1 mark* |
| **c** | very unlikely | *1 mark* |
| **d** | certain | *1 mark* |
| | | **Total 4 marks** |

**4** Shape (c) is similar to the shaded shape. *1 mark*
Shape (e) is congruent to the shaded shape. *1 mark*
**Total 2 marks**

### Examiner's tip
Remember, 'similar' means same shape, different size; 'congruent' means exactly the same shape and size.

| | | |
|---|---|---:|
| **5a** | £69 | *1 mark* |
| **b** | $C = 9d + 15$ | *1 mark* |
| **c** | 9 | *1 mark* |
| | | **Total 3 marks** |

### Examiner's tip
Do not include the £ sign in your formula, since all the parts are in pounds. You must subtract 15 before dividing by 9 in part c.

52

# Test A Answers

| | | |
|---|---|---|
| **6a** | 4860 | *1 mark* |
| **b** | 30 | *1 mark* |
| **c** | 100 | *1 mark* |
| **d** | 5160 | *1 mark* |
| **e** | 400 | *1 mark* |
| **f** | 3.28 | *1 mark* |
| **g** | 1000 | *1 mark* |
| **h** | 13 | *1 mark* |
| | | **Total 8 marks** |

### Examiner's tip

Remember that a number moves to the left one space every time you multiply by 10, and one to the right when you divide by 10.

| | | |
|---|---|---|
| **7a** | Between 70 and 80 kilograms | *1 mark* |
| **b** | Between 6 and 8 metres | *1 mark* |
| **c** | Between 20 and 25 feet | *1 mark* |
| **d** | 4 to 5 | *1 mark* |
| | | **Total 4 marks** |

### Examiner's tip

A rough conversion for pounds is 2 pounds to 1 kg, although 2.2 pounds is more accurate. There are just over 3 feet in 1 metre. One litre is about $1\frac{3}{4}$ pints.

| | | |
|---|---|---|
| **8** | Brand B | *1 mark* |
| | Although a lower mean it has a much narrower range. | *1 mark* |
| | | **Total 2 marks** |

### Examiner's tip

Although Brand A lasts longer on average, some of them will not last as long as those in Brand B. Brand B are more reliable/consistent. If you bought a lot of batteries, Brand A would be better.

| | | |
|---|---|---|
| **9a** | £7.65 | *2 marks* |
| **b** | £6.12 | *2 marks* |
| | | **Total 4 marks** |

### Examiner's tip

In each part there will be one mark for a correct method, e.g.,

$$\begin{array}{r} 45 \\ \times 17 \\ \hline 450 \\ 315 \end{array}$$

and multiplying by 0.8 for part **b**.

# Test A Answers

**10**  558 + 42 = 600  *2 marks*
**Total 2 marks**

> **Examiner's tip**
>
> 2 marks if all correct. Award 1 mark if the digits in the units column add to 10.

**11a** (i)  $\frac{1}{5}$ or 0.2 or 20%  *1 mark*
  (ii)  $\frac{3}{5}$ or 0.6 or 60%  *1 mark*
 **b** (i)  Too few results to be reliable  *1 mark*
  (ii)  $\frac{23}{100}$ or 0.23 or 23%  *1 mark*
 **c** (i)  0.25  *1 mark*
  (ii)  0.75  *1 mark*
**Total 6 marks**

> **Examiner's tip**
>
> These answers show the only acceptable ways of writing probabilities. The answers to part **c** are found by subtracting from 1.

**12a** (i)  10   (ii) $2n$  *1 + 1 marks*
 **b** (i)  9    (ii) $2n - 1$  *1 + 1 marks*
 **c** (i)  19   (ii) $4n - 1$  *1 + 1 marks*
 **d**  $2n + (2n - 1) = 4n - 1$  *1 mark*
**Total 7 marks**

> **Examiner's tip**
>
> If you add the corresponding terms of the first two sequences you get the third.

**13a**  £300, £450  *2 marks*
 **b**  25%  *2 marks*
**Total 4 marks**

> **Examiner's tip**
>
> In part **a**, using two or three fifths will earn one mark and in part **b** dividing 150 by 600 will earn one mark.

**14a**  View 2  *1 mark*
 **b**  *2 marks*

**Total 3 marks**

> **Examiner's tip**
>
> In part **b**, there will be one mark for the correct shape of the outline, one mark for the roof tops and one mark for the joins of the roofs.

54

# Test B Answers

| | | |
|---|---|---|
| **15a** | 25% | *1 mark* |
| **b** | 125 (people) | *1 mark* |
| **c** | Not correct because although percentages are similar, the number of people interviewed is not the same. | *1 mark* |
| **d** | The same percentage of people surveyed in both towns. | *1 mark* |
| | | **Total 4 marks** |

> **Examiner's tip**
>
> The wording in parts **c** and **d** can be different but the argument/reason must mention the different sample sizes.

**TEST TOTAL 60 MARKS**

## TEST B  Pages 13–22

**1**  A: 5  B: 6
    C: 2  D: 4

*1 mark for each answer: 4 marks*
**Total 4 marks**

> **Examiner's tip**
>
> To find the order of rotational symmetry, count how many times the object fits on itself as you turn it. Don't forget to include the original position.

| | | |
|---|---|---|
| **2a** | £3.12 | *1 mark* |
| **b** | 18p | *1 mark* |
| **c** | £12.38 | *1 mark* |
| **d (i)** | $\frac{2}{3}$ | *1 mark* |
| **(ii)** | 50% | *1 mark* |
| **(iii)** | £6.06 | *1 mark* |
| | | **Total 6 marks** |

> **Examiner's tip**
>
> You could have left your answer to part **d(i)** as $\frac{52}{78}$ but it is better to give the simplest equivalent fraction – its size is more easily appreciated.

| | | |
|---|---|---|
| **3a** | 152.5 | *1 mark* |
| **b** | Frequency: 6, 6, 10, 5, 3. | *2 marks* |
| **c** | Bar graph (bars across 130–140, 140–150, etc) or a polygon (points at 135, 145, etc.) | *1 mark* |
| | Heights plotted the same as your answer to part **b** | *1 mark* |
| **d** | 150 to 159 | *1 mark* |
| **e** | Ranjit's class has a higher modal group. | *1 mark* |
| | the shortest pupils are in Ranjit's class or the tallest are in the other class. | *1 mark* |
| | | **Total 8 marks** |

> **Examiner's tip**
>
> As there are an even number of heights, the median is between the middle two, 152 and 153. Your comparisons in part **e** should be about the heights, not the shape of the graph.

# Test B Answers

4a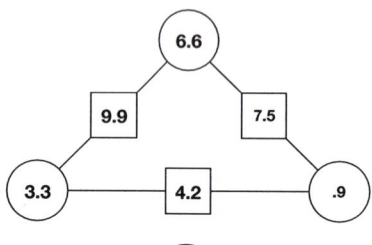

1 mark

b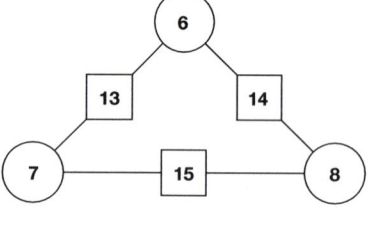

2 marks for all 3 correct, 1 mark for 2 correct

c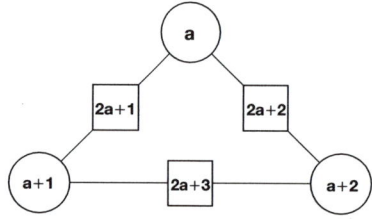

2 marks for all 3 correct, 1 mark for 2 correct

**Total 5 marks**

### Examiner's tip

Check by adding your answers in the circles at the end of each line.

5a    Three angles and two sides accurately drawn      4 marks
b    Angle = 66°      1 mark
     Other sides = 7.9 and 5.4 cm (or 79 and 54 m, full size)      1 mark

**Total 6 marks**

### Examiner's tip

Ask someone to check the accuracy of your drawing. The angles should be within 1° and the lengths within 1 mm of the stated sizes. If you have drawn it accurately, you should get these other measurements, to the same accuracy.

6a (i)    Straight line passing through (0, 1) and (4, 9)      1 + 1 marks
 (ii)    Straight line passing through (0, 3) and (3, 0)      1 + 1 marks
b    (0.7, 2.3)      1 mark

**Total 5 marks**

### Examiner's tip

Your lines should be ruled carefully and reach at least as far as the points indicated. If drawn accurately the lines will meet at the given point, reading to the nearest 0.1.

# Test B Answers

| | | | |
|---|---|---|---|
| **7a** | £7560 | | *1 mark* |
| **b** | £2940 | | *1 mark* |
| **c** | £1996.26 | | *1 mark* |
| **d** | $20\,000 \times 0.1 \times 1 = 2000$ | | *2 marks* |
| | | | **Total 5 marks** |

### Examiner's tip

There are other possible answers to part **d**. Make the numbers as simple as possible but without moving too far from the original size. One way to do this is shown. Since 0.14 is multiplied by 0.679, making one smaller and the other larger keeps the result about right. You will score one mark for an attempt to round the numbers, e.g., $21\,000 \times 0.15 \times 0.68$ – but not easy to work out in the head!

| | | |
|---|---|---|
| **8** | $1000 \div 230 = 4.35$ | *1 mark* |
| | 5 amp | *1 mark* |
| | | **Total 2 marks** |

### Examiner's tip

Show the result of your calculation as well as the size of the fuse.

| | | |
|---|---|---|
| **9a** | Rhombus | *1 mark* |
| **b** | Rectangle | *1 mark* |
| **c** | Trapezium | *1 mark* |
| **d** | Kite (or arrowhead) | *1 mark* |
| | | **Total 4 marks** |

### Examiner's tip

Apart from part **d**, there is only one answer in each case. An arrowhead is not a convex polygon but it has the same properties as a kite.

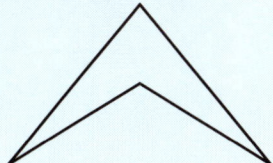

| | | |
|---|---|---|
| **10a** | $x = 3$ | *1 mark* |
| **b** | $2x = -12$ | *1 mark* |
| | $x = -6$ | *1 mark* |
| **c** | $3 = 3x$ or $-3x = -3$ | *1 mark* |
| | $x = 1$ | *1 mark* |
| | | **Total 5 marks** |

### Examiner's tip

The correct solutions will earn both marks in parts **b** and **c**. However, it is a good idea to write down all the steps in the solution to equations, in case you make a mistake.

## Test B Answers

| | | | |
|---|---|---|---|
| **11a** | 11 (millimetres) | | *1 mark* |
| **b** | 0 (millimetres) | | *1 mark* |
| **c** | 1.5 (millimetres) | | *2 marks* |
| **d** | 2.8 (millimetres) | | *1 mark* |
| **e** | Median – e.g. because it ignores the high value. | | |
| | or Mean – e.g. because it gives a good indication of the amount of rain. | | *1 mark* |
| | | | **Total 6 marks** |

### Examiner's tip

In **e** the mode is not a good average to use as only 4 days had no rain. Either median or mean with a valid reason would gain the mark.

| | | |
|---|---|---|
| **12a** | £70 | *2 marks* |
| **b** | 28.6% | *2 marks* |
| | | **Total 4 marks** |

### Examiner's tip

In each part there is a mark for the method if you got the answer wrong, e.g., $50 + \frac{2}{5} \times 50$ and $\frac{20}{70} \times 100$. Remember to use the price before the sale in part **b**.

**TEST TOTAL 60 MARKS**

## TEST C  Pages 23–30

| | | |
|---|---|---|
| **1a** | Four axes | *1 mark* |
| | Order 4 | *1 mark* |
| **b** | Two axes | *1 mark* |
| | Order 2 | *1 mark* |
| **c** | Rhombus | |

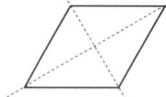

| | |
|---|---|
| | *1 mark* |
| | **Total 5 marks** |

### Examiner's tip

The shape in part **c** does not have to be a quadrilateral, as the answer to part **b** shows!

| | | |
|---|---|---|
| **2a** | 17 | *1 mark* |
| **b** | 6.3 | *1 mark* |
| | | **Total 2 marks** |

### Examiner's tip

In part **b**, 13 must be added to the 50 before dividing by 10.

## Test C Answers

| | | |
|---|---|---|
| 3a | 3 (Weather data previously collected) | 1 mark |
| b | 1 (1 divided by the number of possibilities, about 0.000 000 07) | 1 mark |
| c | 2 (drop a drawing pin 100 times) | 1 mark |
| d | 3 | 1 mark |
| | | **Total 4 marks** |

### Examiner's tip
The method in part **d** will not be very reliable!

| | | |
|---|---|---|
| 4a | $x = 2\frac{1}{2}$ | 1 mark |
| b | $2x + 6 = 5$ or $x + 3 = 2\frac{1}{2}$ | 1 mark |
| | $x = -\frac{1}{2}$ | 1 mark |
| c | $4 - 7x = 3x - 30$ | 1 mark |
| | $x = 3.4$ | 1 mark |
| d | $-x > -1$ or $1 > x$ | 1 mark |
| | $x < 1$ | 1 mark |
| | | **Total 7 marks** |

### Examiner's tip
Great care is needed with the negative signs in part **d**. $1 > x$ is a satisfactory solution but it is usual to finish with $x$ on the left.

| | | |
|---|---|---|
| 5a | 17 | 2 marks |
| b | $P = 4n + 20$ | 1 mark |
| c | $4n + 20 = 20 + \dfrac{n^2}{10}$ | 1 mark |
| | $n = 40$ | 1 mark |
| | | **Total 5 marks** |

### Examiner's tip
Remember to show the method in part **a**. The answer is not 16 as she will not have reached £250 by then, only £240. There is another solution in part **c**, $n = 0$ (they both start with £20).

| | | |
|---|---|---|
| 6a | Finding lengths 5 and 19 | 1 mark |
| | 60 | 1 mark |
| b | $3x^2 = 1200$ | 1 mark |
| | $x^2 = 400$ | 1 mark |
| | 20 and 60 | 1 mark |
| | | **Total 5 marks** |

### Examiner's tip
You could guess the dimensions of the rectangles in part **a**, assuming they were all whole numbers. However, it is better to be systematic: the square has side 5; 95 ÷ 5 = 19; 228 ÷ 19 = 12. You will not get full marks in part **b** if you only give the answer. The question asks for a solution by algebra.

# Test C Answers

| | | |
|---|---|---|
| **7a** | 138°; angles on a straight line add to 180° | 1 + 1 marks |
| **b** | 37°; corresponding angles between BC and ED | 1 + 1 marks |
| **c** | 101°; angles of a triangle add to 180° | 1 + 1 marks |
| | | **Total 6 marks** |

### Examiner's tip

Don't be tempted to measure the angles on the test paper, as they are far from accurate! Use the information given.

| | | |
|---|---|---|
| **8a (i)** | 123, 132, 213, 231, 312, 321 | 2 marks |
| **(ii)** | $\frac{1}{6}$ | 1 mark |
| **b (i)** | 107, 170, 116, 161, 125, 152, 134, 143 | 2 marks |
| **(ii)** | $\frac{1}{6}$ | 1 mark |
| **(iii)** | $\frac{3}{6}$ or $\frac{1}{2}$ | 1 mark |
| | | **Total 7 marks** |

### Examiner's tip

You may make one error and still score one mark in each of parts **a(i)** and **b(i)**. Be systematic in writing them down as this will help you not to miss one or repeat one, both of which will lose a mark. In part **b(ii)**, two combinations have one repeated so are not included when calculating the probability.

| | | |
|---|---|---|
| **9a** | $\frac{13}{24}$, $\frac{5}{8}\left(=\frac{15}{24}\right)$, $\frac{2}{3}\left(=\frac{16}{24}\right)$, $\frac{5}{6}\left(=\frac{20}{24}\right)$ | 1 mark correct equivalent fractions, 1 mark for correct order *2 marks* |
| **b (i)** | $\frac{16}{24} + \frac{15}{24} =$ | 1 mark |
| | $\frac{31}{24}$ or $1\frac{7}{24}$ | 1 mark |
| **(ii)** | $\frac{2 \times 5}{3 \times 8} = \frac{10}{24}$ | 1 mark |
| | $= \frac{5}{12}$ | 1 mark |
| | | **Total 6 marks** |

### Examiner's tip

The methods for combining fractions are shown above and earn marks.

| | | |
|---|---|---|
| **10** | Area of trapezium = 120 cm² | 1 mark |
| | Volume = 120 × 100 = 12 000 cm³ | 1 + 1 marks |
| | | **Total 3 marks** |

### Examiner's tip

Use the formulae sheet on page 70 for the area of the trapezium and the volume of the prism.

## Test D Answers

**11a** Dividing by a number less than 1 increases the size of a number — *1 mark*
**b (i)** 16 — *1 mark*
**(ii)** 0.51 — *1 mark*
**(iii)** 160 — *1 mark*
**(iv)** 0.016 — *1 mark*
**Total 5 marks**

### Examiner's tip
Notice that the square root of a number less than 1 is larger than the original number.

**12a** Scatter graph plotted — *2 marks*

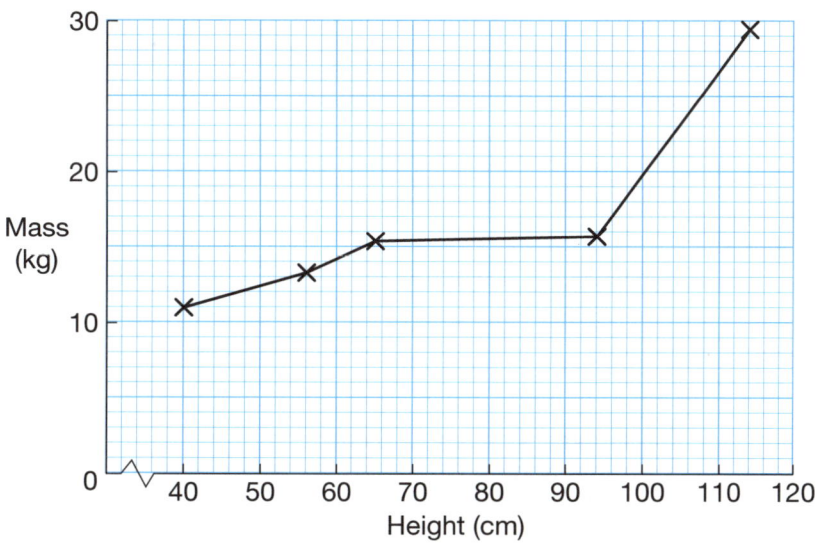

**b** Positive — *1 mark*
**c** Between 80 and 100 — *1 mark*
Read from a line of best fit or from the nearest point — *1 mark*
**Total 5 marks**

### Examiner's tip
It is not a strong positive correlation. A line of best fit will tend to ignore the point for the King penguin. If you use this for part **c**, your answer should be near 80.

**TEST TOTAL 60 MARKS**

### TEST D  Pages 31–39

**1**  15 to 30 cm   4 to 6 m — *1 + 1 marks*
     1 to 2 kg   8 to 15 g — *1 + 1 marks*
**Total 4 marks**

### Examiner's tip
You can check these afterwards but be careful with the bus!

# Test D Answers

| | | | |
|---|---|---|---|
| **2a** | | Proportion of Forest and Grazing about the same | *1 mark* |
| | | More Arable in Europe or more Non-productive in North America | *1 mark* |
| **b** | | The total area of North America is not the same as the total area of Europe | *1 mark* |
| | | | **Total 3 marks** |

### Examiner's tip

You may have some different answers in part **a**. When asked to make two comparisons, look for what is the same and what is different.

| | | | |
|---|---|---|---|
| **3a** | (i) | The rhombus is half a rectangle measuring $x$ by $y$. | *1 mark* |
| | (ii) | 59.5 cm$^2$ | *1 mark* |
| | (iii) | 5.6 | *1 mark* |
| **b** | (i) | $x + x + 2 + x + x + 2$ | *1 mark* |
| | | $4x + 4$ or $4(x + 1)$ | *1 mark* |
| | (ii) | 100 | *1 mark* |
| | (iii) | 0.25 or $\frac{1}{4}$ | *1 mark* |
| | | | **Total 7 marks** |

### Examiner's tip

The simplified expression will earn both marks in part **b(i)**.

| | | | |
|---|---|---|---|
| **4a** | 150 cm | | *1 mark* |
| **b** | 800 mm | | *1 mark* |
| **c** | Accurate drawing: | lengths 4 cm and 7.5 cm | *1 mark* |
| | | Right angles | *1 mark* |
| | | Semicircle radius 2 cm | *1 mark* |
| **d** | $\frac{1}{2} \times \pi \times 0.8$ for semicircle | | *1 mark* |
| | 5.06 m | | *1 mark* |
| **e** | $\frac{1}{2} \times \pi \times 0.4^2$ | | *1 mark* |
| | $0.8 \times 1.5$ | | *1 mark* |
| | 1.451 m$^2$ | | *1 mark* |
| | | | **Total 10 marks** |

### Examiner's tip

The answers to parts **d** and **e** are given correct to three significant figures. You would not lose marks here for giving more figures but it would not be sensible from the measurements given in the question.

| | | |
|---|---|---|
| **5** | $6.59 \div 7.5 = 0.879$ | *1 mark* |
| | $2.59 \div 3 = 0.863$ | *1 mark* |
| | $0.65 \div 0.69 = 0.942$ | *1 mark* |
| | The 3 kg is best as it costs less per kilogram | *1 mark* |
| | | **Total 4 marks** |

### Examiner's tip

You could instead calculate how much washing powder you get for £1 or 1p. The largest number will then represent the best buy.

# Test D Answers

| | | |
|---|---|---|
| **6a** | $90 \times 11 \div 16$ | *1 mark* |
| | 61.875, or 61.9 or 62 | *1 mark* |
| **b** | $24 \times 16 \div 11$ | *1 mark* |
| | 34.9 or 35 | *1 mark* |
| | | **Total 4 marks** |

> **Examiner's tip**
>
> The data in the question is to the nearest centimetre/millimetre, so similar accuracy is sensible for the answers. Notice that it is not necessary to convert the millimetres into centimetres in part **b**, as the question is about proportion.

| | | |
|---|---|---|
| **7a** | (Strong) positive correlation | *1 mark* |
| **b** | Negative correlation | *1 mark* |
| **c** | P (or possibly S) | *1 mark* |
| **d** | Q | *1 mark* |
| | | **Total 4 marks** |

| | | |
|---|---|---|
| **8a** | 29 | *1 mark* |
| **b** | $2 + 3(n - 1)$ or $3n - 1$ | *1 mark* |
| | | **Total 2 marks** |

> **Examiner's tip**
>
> It helps to write out the position and term values in a row:
>
> Position  1   2   3   4 ...
> Term      2   5   8   11 ...

| | | |
|---|---|---|
| **9a** | $\dfrac{23\,720}{24 \times 24} = 41.18\,\text{km/h}$ | *2 marks* |
| **b** | e.g. 'Average' walking speed is 6 km/h | *1 mark* |
| | Drive speed is approximately 42 km/h | |
| | Ratio of speeds = 42:6 = 7:1 | |
| | Ratio of times = 1:7 | |
| | Therefore walking takes $7 \times 24 = 168$ days | *2 marks* |
| | | **Total 5 marks** |

> **Examiner's tip**
>
> In **b** the time would be a guide to the minimum. There is a range of possible assumptions. Examiners would give credit for sensible assumptions and a time between 160 and 240 days.

| | | |
|---|---|---|
| **10a** | Using midpoints 5, 15, 25, 35, 45, 55, 65 | *1 mark* |
| | Multiplying these by the frequencies, adding and dividing by 120 | *1 mark* |
| | 35.7 years | *1 mark* |
| **b** | 29 or 30 years | *1 mark* |
| | Median between 60th and 61st, at top of group 20 to 30 | *1 mark* |
| **c** | Second more evenly distributed, or less old people | *1 mark* |
| | Mean is almost the same | *1 mark* |
| | | **Total 7 marks** |

# Test D Answers

> **Examiner's tip**
>
> When the mean and the median are about the same size, the distribution is balanced and not weighted to an extreme. In the first case here, the 26 people over 60 caused the mean to be higher than the median.

**11**  $\sqrt{51^2 - 27^2}$ — *1 mark*
$\sqrt{1872} \times 27 \div 2$ — *1 mark*
584 — *1 mark*
**Total 3 marks**

> **Examiner's tip**
>
> In this question you have to recognise that the third side is needed to find the area and that Pythagoras is the way to find it. The correct answer would earn all three marks.

**12a**  Multiply one equation appropriately, i.e. $6x + 9y = -9$ or $18x - 3y = 33$ — *1 mark*
Obtain equation in one unknown, i.e. $10y = -20$ or $20x = 30$ — *1 mark*
$x = 1\frac{1}{2}, y = -2$ — *1 mark*
  **b (i)**  2 — *1 mark*
    **(ii)**  Trial between 2 and 2.5 — *1 mark*
Trial between 2.25 and 2.3 — *1 mark*
2.28 — *1 mark*
**Total 7 marks**

> **Examiner's tip**
>
> To decide between 2.27 (value 4.887) and 2.28 (value 5.012), work out the value for 2.275, which is 4.949, so it is higher than 2.275.

**TEST TOTAL 60 MARKS**

# Test E Answers

## TEST E  Pages 40–48

**1a**  $8 \times \dfrac{8}{5}$ cm — *1 mark*

   $= 12.8$ cm — *1 mark*

**b**  $5 \times \dfrac{5}{8}$ feet — *1 mark*

   $= 3\tfrac{1}{8}$ or $3.125$ feet — *1 mark*

   **Total 4 marks**

### Examiner's tip
Not a very sensible scale! As a check, notice that it is 1.6 cm to one foot. That means that the number of centimetres on the model should be greater than the number of feet on the real tent.

**2**  Total weight of men = 750 kg
   Total weight of women = 750 kg — *1 mark*
   $1500 \div 25$ — *1 mark*
   $= 60$ kg — *1 mark*

   **Total 3 marks**

### Examiner's tip
An alternative method is to calculate $\tfrac{2}{5} \times 75 + \tfrac{3}{5} \times 50$, that is as a proportion calculation.

**3a**  $\dfrac{60 \times 20}{30} = 40$ — *1 mark*

**b**  $\dfrac{0.7 \times 60}{10}$ or $\dfrac{0.8 \times 50}{10}$ — *1 mark*

   $= 4$

   **Total 2 marks**

### Examiner's tip
Try to choose approximations that make the arithmetic easy. Only give one significant figure in your answer.

**4a**  $7 \times \tfrac{3}{5} = 4\tfrac{1}{5}$ — *1 mark*
   5 tins needed — *1 mark*

**b**  $\tfrac{3}{4} \times 600$ — *1 mark*
   $= 450$ — *1 mark*

**c**  $\tfrac{3}{5} + \tfrac{1}{4} = \tfrac{12 + 5}{20}$ — *1 mark*
   $= \tfrac{17}{20}$ — *1 mark*

   **Total 6 marks**

### Examiner's tip
If you got any of these fractions wrong, you need some more practice!

# Test E Answers

**5a**   $\frac{1}{6}$   *1 mark*

  **b**   0.3   *1 mark*

  **c (i)**   $\frac{1}{6} \times 0.1 = \frac{1}{60}$   *1 mark*

    **(ii)**   $\frac{1}{6} \times 0.9 + \frac{5}{6} \times 0.1$   *1+1 mark*

       $\frac{9}{60} + \frac{5}{60} = \frac{14}{60} = \frac{7}{30}$   *1 mark*

**Total 6 marks**

### Examiner's tip
It is easier to work in fractions here. Notice that in part **c(ii)** there are two possibilities – Dillon gets a 6 but Karl does not and vice versa. As these are alternatives (and exclusive) the probabilities are added.

**6a** 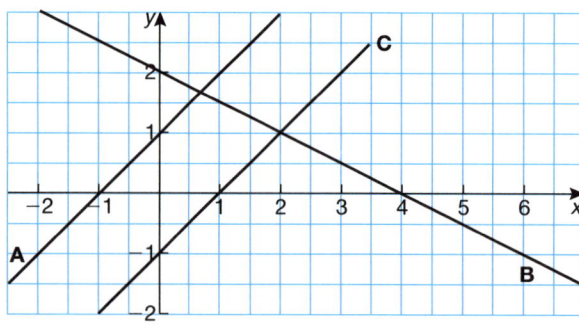   *1 mark*

  **b**   $x + 2y$   *1 mark*

     $= 4$   *1 mark*

  **c**   Taking reading where A and B meet   *1 mark*

     $x = 0.7, y = 1.7$   *1 mark*

**Total 5 marks**

### Examiner's tip
If you wanted to (and you had time!), you could check your answer by algebra. This solution is $x = \frac{2}{3}, y = 1\frac{2}{3}$.

**7a**   $a^5$   *1 mark*

  **b**   $12a^9$   *1 mark*

  **c**   $a^5 b^3$   *1 mark*

  **d**   $x^6$   *1 mark*

  **e**   $a^4 b^2 c^6$   *1 mark*

  **f**   1   *1 mark*

**Total 6 marks**

### Examiner's tip
Remember in part **f** – anything raised to the power of 0 is 1.

# Test E Answers

8

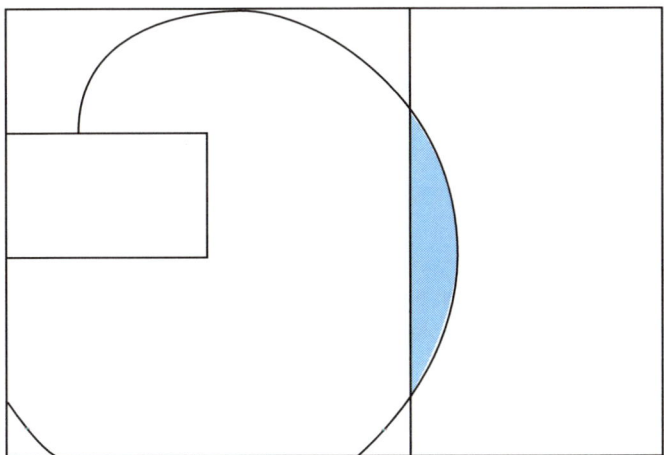

| | | |
|---|---|---|
| a | Straight line 5 cm from rail | 1 mark |
| b | (Part) circle radius 5 cm | 1 mark |
| | Quarter circle radius 2.5 cm | 1 mark |
| c | Segment shaded blue | 1 mark |
| | | **Total 4 marks** |

### Examiner's tip

Ruler, compasses and sharp pencil are needed to answer this question. Don't obliterate your drawing with the shading.

9

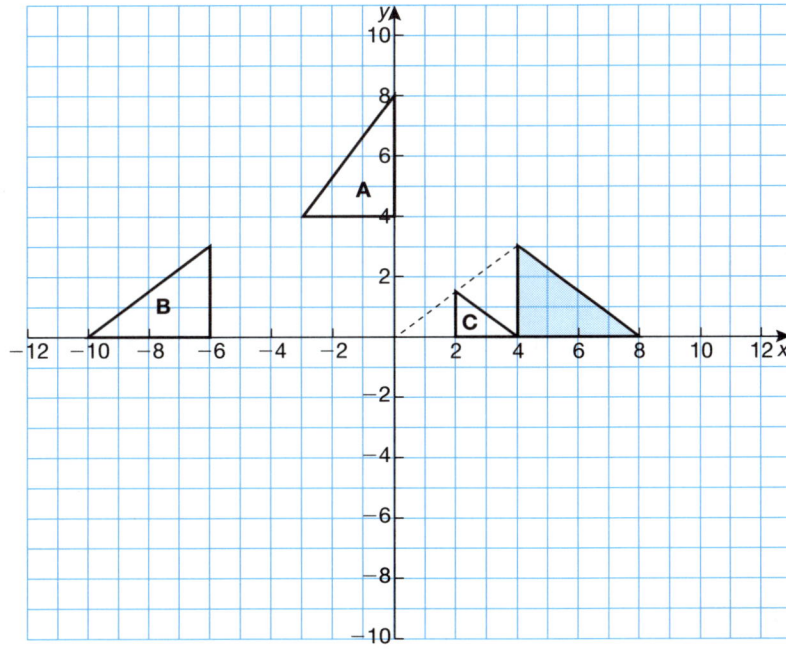

*Two marks for each correct action: 6 marks*
**Total 6 marks**

### Examiner's tip

There are two marks for each part. Any error will lose one mark.

# Test E Answers

**10a**    $3x - 6 + 8x - 12$    *1 mark*
       $= 11x - 18$    *1 mark*
**b**    $10x^2 - 15x$    *1 mark*
**c**    $2x^2 + 5x - 3x^2 + 6x$    *1 mark*
       $= -x^2 + 11x$    *1 mark*
       **Total 5 marks**

### Examiner's tip

If you wrote down the answers correctly in one step each time you will get all the marks. However, it is worth writing down the intermediate steps in case you make an error.

**11a**    Median = 6.0    *1 mark*
**b**    Quartiles = 4.5 and 6.7    *1 mark*
       Interquartile range = 2.2    *1 mark*
**c**    1:F    2:D    3:B    4:G    *3 marks*
       **Total 6 marks**

### Examiner's tip

Even if you read the quartiles wrongly, you could get one mark for subtracting them. Each error in part **c** will lose a mark. If the median is higher, the middle of the graph will be further to the right. If the interquartile range is larger the graph will be less steep.

**12a**    $(x + 8)^2 = x^2 + (x + 7)^2$    *1 mark*
**b**    $x^2 - 2x$    *1 mark*
       $-15 = 0$    *1 mark*
**c**    $(x - 5)(x + 3) = 0$    *1 mark*
       $x = 5$ or $x = -3$    *1 mark*
       **Total 5 marks**

### Examiner's tip

The solution of the equation gives two values for *x*, both of which you should have given. However, had you been asked to find the lengths of the sides of the triangle, $x = -3$ is not a possible value, so $x = 5$ gives the lengths 5, 12, 13.

**13**    $\dfrac{6 + x}{6} = \dfrac{15}{10}$    *1 mark*
       $x = 3$    *1 mark*
       **Total 2 marks**

### Examiner's tip

The two parallel lines create similar triangles (corresponding angles are equal). The equation comes from the ratio of corresponding sides being equal.

**TEST TOTAL 60 MARKS**

# Mental Test Answers

## MENTAL TEST 1

| | | | | | |
|---|---|---|---|---|---|
| 1 | 19 | 11 | 2.5 | 21 | 25 |
| 2 | 56 | 12 | 0.04 | 22 | 120 |
| 3 | 2500 | 13 | 20 | 23 | $\frac{11}{15}$ |
| 4 | 10 000 | 14 | $\frac{1}{8}$ or 0.125 | 24 | 18 |
| 5 | 75 | 15 | 4300 | 25 | £4000 |
| 6 | 18 | 16 | $x = 1$ or 0 | 26 | 2 |
| 7 | 15 | 17 | 78° | 27 | 25% |
| 8 | 600 | 18 | 16 | 28 | 12 |
| 9 | 30 cm | 19 | 32 | 29 | 70.3 |
| 10 | $x = 8$ | 20 | 30 kg | 30 | $\frac{85}{100}$ or $\frac{17}{20}$ |

## MENTAL TEST 2

| | | | | | |
|---|---|---|---|---|---|
| 1 | 4 | 11 | $-1$ | 21 | 6 cm$^2$ |
| 2 | 1.8 | 12 | $\frac{1}{100}$ | 22 | 8 |
| 3 | 750 | 13 | 9 | 23 | 249 |
| 4 | 9 | 14 | 0.95 | 24 | 10 m |
| 5 | 210 | 15 | 45 | 25 | 87° |
| 6 | 0.65 | 16 | 7 minutes 30 seconds | 26 | $\frac{6}{150}$ or $\frac{1}{25}$ |
| 7 | 3.02 | 17 | $\frac{1}{6}$ | 27 | 17 |
| 8 | 12 | 18 | e.g., $-11, -20, -10.1$ | 28 | 0.0243 89 |
| 9 | $2x$ hours | 19 | Between 2 and 3 cm | 29 | 22.5 s |
| 10 | 7 | 20 | 20% | 30 | Perpendicular bisector of line joining buoys |

### Examiner's tip

You must listen carefully. 'Sixty' can sound like 'sixteen' if you are not concentrating. Ten seconds may not sound very long but, with practice, you should be able to answer questions like this in that time in your head. To get some more practice, ask someone to make up other questions like these, but with different numbers. Your score should soon improve – your target is to get them all right!

# Formulae

You might need these two formulae. For π, use the value of π given on your calculator.
If your calculator does not have a π button, use π = 3.142.

| AREA | VOLUME |

**Trapezium**

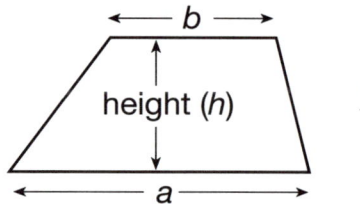

$$\frac{(a+b)}{2} \times h$$

**Prism**

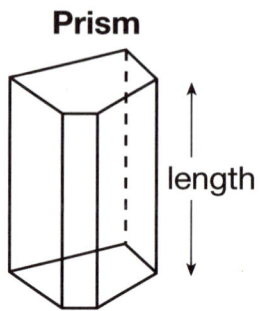

area of cross-section × length

# Mental Test 1 Questions

**INSTRUCTIONS**

Detach this page from the book.
Read each question, exactly as printed, twice.
Allow a short time for each answer to be written down (on page 49)
For questions 1 to 6, allow 5 seconds; questions 7 to 20, allow 10 seconds and for questions 21 to 30, allow 15 seconds.

1. Subtract eighteen from thirty-seven.
2. What number, divided by seven, gives eight?
3. How many millilitres are there in two and a half litres?
4. What is one hundred squared?
5. How many minutes is it from eleven fifteen to twelve thirty?
6. Two $x$ equals thirty-six. What is $x$?

7. $x$ minus $y$ is three. What is five $x$ minus five $y$?
8. What is the approximate value of the expression on your answer sheet?
9. Circle the measurement that is about the same as one foot.
10. Solve the equation on the answer sheet.
11. A tree trunk is twelve point five metres long. It is cut into five equal pieces. How long is each?
12. Work out nought point two squared.
13. What is two percent of one thousand?
14. What is the probability that a fair coin will land heads three times in a row?
15. Write the number four thousand, three hundred and forty-nine correct to two significant figures.
16. Solve the equation on your answer sheet.
17. Two angles of a triangle are sixty-five degrees and thirty-seven degrees. What is the third?
18. The mean of five numbers is ten. Another number is included. The new mean is eleven. What is the other number?
19. A bottle of milk will fill two and a half glasses. How many bottles are needed to fill eighty glasses?
20. Circle the mass that could be that of a holiday suitcase.

21. Find the median of the numbers on your answer sheet.
22. A car travelled two hundred and ten kilometres in one and three-quarter hours. What was its average speed?
23. Add the fractions on your answer sheet.
24. The pie chart shows how thirty pupils came to school. About how many walked?
25. A block of precious metal measures five by four by two centimetres. It costs one hundred pounds a cubic centimetre. How much is the block worth?
26. Work out nought point two divided by nought point one.
27. What is thirty as a percentage of one hundred and twenty?
28. What is the length of the third side of the triangle on your answer sheet?
29. Seven hundred and three divided by nineteen is thirty-seven. What is three point seven times nineteen?
30. Write down a fraction equal to nought point eight five.

# Mental Test 2 Questions

**INSTRUCTIONS**

Detach this page from the book.
Read each question, exactly as printed, twice.
Allow a short time for each answer to be written down (on page 50)
For questions 1 to 6, allow 5 seconds; questions 7 to 20, allow 10 seconds and for questions 21 to 30, allow 15 seconds.

1. Divide ten by five and then add two.
2. Work out three point seven minus one point nine.
3. How many centimetres are there in seven and a half metres?
4. Divide seventy-two by eight.
5. Multiply two by three by five by seven.
6. What number is one hundred times bigger than nought point nought six five?

7. Write the number three point nought one seven correct to two decimal places.
8. How many edges has a cube?
9. A car travelling at one hundred kilometres an hour completes a journey in $x$ hours. How long will it take to complete the journey at fifty kilometres an hour.
10. What is the value of five $x$ minus three when $x$ equals two?
11. Write down the next number in the sequence fourteen, nine, four, …
12. What is ten grams as a fraction of a kilogram?
13. The ratio of apples to oranges in a fruit bowl is two to three. There are six apples. How many oranges are there?
14. The probability that my train will be late is nought point nought five. What is the probability that it will be on time?
15. Find one hundred and fifty percent of thirty.
16. I made three telephone calls lasting one minute thirty five seconds, five minutes and three seconds and fifty-two seconds. What was the total time?
17. Write the fraction on the answer sheet in its lowest terms.
18. Write down a value of $x$ which satisfies the inequality on your answer sheet.
19. Estimate the length of the line on your answer sheet.
20. The price of a ticket falls from £5 to £4. What percentage reduction is this?

21. Work out the area of the triangle on your answer sheet.
22. The answer sheet shows the number of points scored by a rugby player in five matches. Find the mean number of points.
23. Use the calculation on your answer sheet to work out how many forty-ones there are in ten thousand two hundred and nine.
24. A circular pond has area seventy-five square metres. Roughly what is its diameter?
25. Three angles of a quadrilateral are one hundred and ten, seventy-three and ninety. What is the fourth angle?
26. Multiply the fractions on your answer sheet.
27. Add together three to the power two and two to the power three.
28. Use the calculation on your answer sheet to work out the value of nought point two nine cubed.
29. Divide three minutes into eight equal parts. How many seconds in each?
30. A pilot steers a ship so that the distances from two marker buoys remain equal. Describe the ship's course.

# Determining your level

**FINDING YOUR LEVEL IN EACH TEST**

When you have completed and marked a test, enter the total number of marks you scored for each question on the Marking Grid overleaf. Then add them up. Using the total for each test, look at the charts below to determine your level for each test.

**Test A or Test B**

| Level 3 or below | Level 4 | Level 5 | Level 6 |
|---|---|---|---|
| up to 13 | 14–26 | 27–39 | 40+ |

After you have worked out separate levels for Tests A and B, add up your total marks for the two tests. Use this total and the chart below to determine your overall level for Tests A and B — this is your level for Mathematics at this point.

**Total for Tests A and B and Mental Test 1**

| Level 3 or below | Level 4 | Level 5 | Level 6 |
|---|---|---|---|
| up to 31 | 32–63 | 64–94 | 95+ |

If your results from Tests A and B indicate that you are working at Level 4 or higher, you should try Tests C and D sometime later. The chart below shows you how to find your level for each of Tests C and D.

**Test C or Test D**

| Level 4 or below | Level 5 | Level 6 | Level 7 or above |
|---|---|---|---|
| up to 15 | 16–24 | 25–42 | 43+ |

**Test E**

| Level 5 or below | Level 6 | Level 7 | Level 8 |
|---|---|---|---|
| up to 13 | 14–24 | 25–41 | 42+ |

**FINDING YOUR OVERALL LEVEL IN MATHEMATICS (WRITTEN TESTS)**

After you have found your level for each test, add up your total marks for Tests C and D. Use this total and the chart below to determine your overall level in Mathematics. The chart also shows you how your level compares with the target level for your age group.

**Total for Tests C and D and Mental Test 2**

| Level 4 or below | Level 5 | Level 6 | Level 7 or above |
|---|---|---|---|
| up to 37 | 38–64 | 65–99 | 100+ |
| Working towards target level | Working at target level for age group | | Working beyond target level |

# Marking grid

### TEST A — Pages 2–12

| Question | Marks available | Marks scored | Question | Marks available | Marks scored | Question | Marks available | Marks scored |
|---|---|---|---|---|---|---|---|---|
| 1 | 3 | | 6 | 8 | | 11 | 6 | |
| 2 | 4 | | 7 | 4 | | 12 | 7 | |
| 3 | 4 | | 8 | 2 | | 13 | 4 | |
| 4 | 2 | | 9 | 4 | | 14 | 3 | |
| 5 | 3 | | 10 | 2 | | 15 | 4 | |
| | | | | | | Total | 60 | |

### TEST B — Pages 13–22

| Question | Marks available | Marks scored | Question | Marks available | Marks scored | Question | Marks available | Marks scored |
|---|---|---|---|---|---|---|---|---|
| 1 | 4 | | 5 | 6 | | 9 | 4 | |
| 2 | 6 | | 6 | 5 | | 10 | 5 | |
| 3 | 8 | | 7 | 5 | | 11 | 6 | |
| 4 | 5 | | 8 | 2 | | 12 | 4 | |
| | | | | | | Total | 60 | |

### TEST C — Pages 23–30

| Question | Marks available | Marks scored | Question | Marks available | Marks scored | Question | Marks available | Marks scored |
|---|---|---|---|---|---|---|---|---|
| 1 | 5 | | 5 | 5 | | 9 | 6 | |
| 2 | 2 | | 6 | 5 | | 10 | 3 | |
| 3 | 4 | | 7 | 6 | | 11 | 5 | |
| 4 | 7 | | 8 | 7 | | 12 | 5 | |
| | | | | | | Total | 60 | |

### TEST D — Pages 31–39

| Question | Marks available | Marks scored | Question | Marks available | Marks scored | Question | Marks available | Marks scored |
|---|---|---|---|---|---|---|---|---|
| 1 | 4 | | 5 | 4 | | 9 | 5 | |
| 2 | 3 | | 6 | 4 | | 10 | 7 | |
| 3 | 7 | | 7 | 4 | | 11 | 3 | |
| 4 | 10 | | 8 | 2 | | 12 | 7 | |
| | | | | | | Total | 60 | |

### TEST E — Pages 40–48

| Question | Marks available | Marks scored | Question | Marks available | Marks scored | Question | Marks available | Marks scored |
|---|---|---|---|---|---|---|---|---|
| 1 | 4 | | 6 | 5 | | 11 | 6 | |
| 2 | 3 | | 7 | 6 | | 12 | 5 | |
| 3 | 2 | | 8 | 4 | | 13 | 2 | |
| 4 | 6 | | 9 | 6 | | | | |
| 5 | 6 | | 10 | 5 | | | | |
| | | | | | | Total | 60 | |

| | Marks available | Marks scored |
|---|---|---|
| Mental Test 1 | 30 | |
| Mental Test 2 | 30 | |